THE **LONE** ARRANGER

SUCCEEDING IN A SMALL REPOSITORY

BY CHRISTINA ZAMON

SOCIETY OF
American
Archivists

CHICAGO

Society of American Archivists
www.archivists.org

@2012 by the Society of American Archivists.
All rights reserved.

Printed in the United States of America

Graphic design by Sweeney Design, kasween@sbcglobal.net

Library of Congress Cataloging-in-Publication Data

Zamon, Christina.
  The lone arranger : succeeding in a small repository / by Christina Zamon.
     p. cm.
  Includes bibliographical references and index.
  ISBN 1-931666-41-5 (alk. paper)
1. Archives—United States—Administration. 2. Archives—Collection management—United States. 3. Archivists—United States. I. Society of American Archivists. II. Title.
  CD950.Z36 2012
  025—dc23
                              2011052238

Acknowledgments

Calls for a book specifically for lone arrangers have been around longer than the span of my archival career. The incredible complexity of situations that lone arrangers face has made writing such a book a challenge that few were willing to undertake and one that I was reluctant to take. I agreed to write this book with the help of many of my colleagues to provide guidance for those who face the daily life of a lone arranger. Not only are we operating archives with little staff and tight budgets, but we must also deal with the current great changes in the nature of archival work as we enter the unknowns of the digital age.

I am greatly indebted to my colleagues for all of their help and support through this process. Having only worked in two types of lone arranger settings, I needed my colleagues' wisdom and expertise to guide me through the challenges that lone arrangers face in the variety of institutions they support. With my colleagues' help I attempted to provide information and knowledge that an archivist could apply to a religious, academic, corporate, government, library, museum, or historical society setting. Throughout the book there are case studies from a variety of lone arrangers working in these settings. My colleagues also provided me with photos and resources that I hope the reader will find useful in understanding how to deal with the daily challenges of being a lone arranger.

Many people helped me through this process and encouraged me to take on this challenge. I would like to thank first and foremost my Lone Arrangers Roundtable colleagues Russ Gasero, Nancy Freeman, Courtney Yevich Tkacz, Colleen McFarland, Alison Stankrauff, and Michelle Ganz for all of their support from the very beginning. I particularly want to thank Colleen and Courtney for being my unofficial editors for the prospectus for this book and Courtney for her continued service as content editor all the way through to the end. I also want to thank Chessie Monks for her incredible work researching my suggested readings list as well as my resources guide. Lone arrangers everywhere wish you much success and hope that you will join our ranks one day.

I would like to thank those individuals and institutions that provided images and case studies. You have provided insight into the daily lives of lone arrangers. Among those individuals are Bob Antonelli, Carol Appenzellar, Barbara Austen, Terry Baxter, Renée DesRoberts, April Gage, Tamara Gaydos, Angela Lembke, Jeremy Linden, Meg Miner, Mary Peters, Christina Prucha, Peg Poeschl Siciliano, John Slate, Nicole Thaxton, Allaina Wallace, Stephanie Williams, Sr. Sally Witt, and Sonia Yaco. I would like to thank the following institutions for allowing me to use their forms and policies as examples: Emerson College, Suffolk University, Diocese of Wilmington Archives, Albuquerque Academy Archives, Santa Ana Public Library, The National Press Club, Jewish Buffalo Archives Project, Montgomery County Historical Society (Maryland), and Wellesley College.

There are a number of people at the Society of American Archivists who provided additional support for my book. I would like to thank my editor, Caryn Radick, who made sense of my ramblings; Peter Wosh and Teresa Brinati, who provided expertise and support throughout this process; and the SAA Publications Board, who gave this project the green light. Without them this book never would have become a reality.

I would like to thank Emerson College for allowing me to pursue this endeavor and providing the support I needed to finish the project. I particularly want to thank Vice President for Academic Affairs Linda Moore, Iwasaki Library Executive Director Robert Fleming, and the rest of my colleagues in the Iwasaki Library.

Last but never least, I want to thank my husband Andrew for his support throughout this entire project, as well as my daughter Rita, who was born in the early stages of this process and is now able to tell me "Turn the [com]'puter off, mommy!" I also want to thank my immediate family, including my parents, my sister, and my in-laws, for their undying love and support. Without their encouragement I wouldn't have the knowledge and expertise to write this book.

CHRISTINA ZAMON

Contents

Introduction

Small repositories and "lone arranger" shops make up a large percentage of archives within the United States. These institutions and their archivists are often underrepresented or overlooked in archival literature. This may be a result of lone arrangers being overburdened with work and unable to take the time to contribute to the larger body of archival literature; it may also be because they feel detached from the larger archival profession. Another issue may be the lack of funding that would allow them to participate in conferences or workshops that would foster a sense of archival community. Some lone arrangers may not even recognize that they are indeed archivists; they may carry titles such as historian, librarian, clerk, or even volunteer. Lone arrangers come from a variety of educational backgrounds and interests that range from formal archival training to a simple passion for history and archives.

This book uses the term "lone arranger" to describe those of us who work alone or with only part-time or volunteer staff. The term "lone arranger" is a play on words from the popular radio and television western, *The Lone Ranger*, in which a single masked man with his trusty steed and Native American sidekick roamed the West fighting crime. Although we are not fighting crime, we are fighting backlogs and the uphill battle to stay on top of our heavy workloads, often without the help of a trusty sidekick.

The biggest challenge in writing a book like this is to tackle all of the exceptions that different lone arrangers face on a daily basis. Not all small shops are created equal. Not only do we work for a wide variety of institutions, but we work part-time, full-time, or as volunteers, or maybe we aren't even "archivists" as defined by our job titles. If you fall into that last category, how do you know if you are an archivist? Do your records fall within the definition of archival records? In the Society of American Archivists' *A Glossary of Archival and Records Terminology,* Richard Pearce-Moses defines these records as "materials created or received by a person, family, or organization, public or private, in the conduct of their affairs that are preserved because of the enduring value contained in the information they contain or as evidence of the functions and responsibilities of their creator."[1] If your work involves maintaining and providing access to these types of records, then you are an archivist.

Whether you have been an archivist for twenty years or you have "accidentally" become an archivist, the information in these pages is intended to provide guidance for the daily challenges your job presents. Given this incredible task, it is impossible to provide detailed information on how to approach every situation an archivist working in a small shop may encounter. This book serves as a guide for those tasked with providing access to archival materials to anyone, including parent organizations, staff, faculty, students, and the general

{ **KEY TERMS**

Lone Arranger: An individual who is the sole staff of an archives.[2]

public. Here you will find tips and ways to deal with common challenges while aspiring to achieve archival best practices. Then it is up to you, the reader, to determine how to proceed in any given situation.

To address the complexity of our jobs, I tried to approach this book from a practical standpoint by focusing on issues of importance to lone arrangers. I thought about the questions archivists would ask as they went about their work. All of these issues are equally important; however, some of us may find certain chapters more relevant to our own work. Each chapter is divided into sections and subsections that make it easier to go directly to a specific topic. This will help you to better understand archival principles and practices as they apply to your work.

Throughout the book you will find case studies written by archivists working in small shops. These case studies provide real-life examples of how lone arrangers have dealt with various aspects of archival work on a daily basis at their institutions. You will also find policies, photographs, and other materials from small repositories across the country that can serve as examples for your own work. This book exemplifies the collaborative nature of lone arrangers and their willingness to share their stories and work with others in an effort to simplify the complex work we face.

Although numerous books have been written on the topics covered here, very few address the day-to-day concerns and issues lone arrangers face. My intent is to provide you with the tools you need to achieve the accepted standards of archival practice to the best of your abilities.

Finally, this book's appendices point to additional literature on specific topics, as well as resources to help with a variety of situations. These resources, including the URLs for websites, were current as of June 2011. Even if a resource's URL changes, you can use the additional information in these appendices to find the resource through a search engine.

NOTES

[1] Richard Pearce-Moses, *A Glossary of Archival and Records Terminology* (Chicago: Society of American Archivists, 2005), available at http://www.archivists.org/glossary/.

[2] Ibid.

CHAPTER 1

"What Am I Doing Here?"

Administration and Management

Getting Started

Welcome to life as an archivist in a small shop or single-person operation! Those archivists who work this way sometimes refer to themselves as "lone arrangers," a term defined by the Society of American Archivists' *A Glossary of Archival and Records Terminology* as "an individual who is the sole staff of an archives." Whether you are part-time or full-time, have volunteers, additional part-time staff, or no staff, you will benefit from the lessons learned by your fellow lone arrangers.

Lone arrangers work for nonprofits, educational institutions, religious institutions, museums, corporations, governments, or any combination of the above. Whether you call yourself an archivist, librarian, secretary, clerk, or records manager, you are the only person responsible for the historical documentation of your organization. You may have part-time assistants, volunteers, or interns or you yourself may be part-time or a volunteer. Perhaps you were hired to start an archives or to formalize an "informal" archives started by a non-archivist. Any way you slice it, you have great responsibilities and wear many hats.

Evaluating the Situation

You may be the first archivist your institution has ever hired. Or you may be the successor of a long line of archivists there. Whatever the situation, you have been given the responsibility to care for the historical records of your institution. Before jumping into your duties, take some time to review any policies that your predecessor or institution has in place regarding the records housed in the archives. In some cases, there may be no existing policies and you will have to look to others for guidance on how to create those.

Before you embark on an ambitious new project, you need to answer several questions about your situation. Start by evaluating your role in the organization.

- What is the significance and/or mandate of your position?

- What is your role? Are you an archivist, manuscripts curator, librarian, museum curator, or volunteer?

- What are your responsibilities?

- Where do you fall within the organizational structure and how much support can you expect from those in positions of authority?

- On whom can you rely for support within your institution?

- If you were hired specifically to run the archives, historical society, museum, or library, do you report to a board of directors, library director, or president?

- Do you have volunteers or assistants?

Once you have answered these questions, you need to determine the status of your institution. You should ask yourself the following questions.

- Why, how, and when was the repository established?

- Were you given a directive from your supervisor(s)? What is that directive?

- Is there an original mission or vision statement for your repository?

- What types of policies are in place? Are the policies outdated due to changes in staff, technology, organizational structure, or other factors?

- How is the institution funded? Will your funding continue, and if so, how?

These questions are important for you to ask as you determine your ultimate goals and priorities. Being the sole archivist is a challenge that requires dedication and determination. It also provides you with varied workdays as you will seldom be able to spend two days in a row doing the exact same thing.

Most archives are founded as a result of a major event, such as a centennial or other celebration. Sometimes archives are started by volunteers, typically non-archivists, and may be a start-and-stop operation until the institution decides that it needs a full-time archivist to establish an archives program.

If you are starting an archives, you should put in place the following basic program elements: planning and administration, collection development, appraisal, records management, collections management, preservation, reference, outreach, and fundraising. All of these elements will be discussed in this book along with several subsets of archival programming. An excellent resource for establishing an archives is Elizabeth Yakel's book *Starting an Archives*.[1]

Managing Your Staff—You!

You are in an unusual, yet not uncommon position as a lone archivist. You may not have a staff to work with, so being a lone arranger means knowing how to manage your time. This is a topic that many archivists may not have considered before. Archivists know how to manage other people, but are they good at managing themselves?

Working alone means not only wearing many hats but juggling those hats to find the right balance. As a lone arranger you need the basic knowledge to do it all without having to master it all. This is no easy feat. Larger archives often have multiple archivists and larger budgets, allowing them to fully process collections, create EAD finding aids, build and create exhibits showcasing their collections, and operate in state-of-the-art buildings. As an archivist in a small shop, you may rarely have the opportunity to experience some of those advantages, and archivists have to adapt their archival skills and training to meet the needs of their organizations while also upholding archival standards to the best of their abilities.

{ KEY TERMS

Encoded Archival Description (EAD) is "a standard used to mark up (encode) finding aids that reflects the hierarchical nature of archival collections and that provides a structure for describing the whole of a collection, as well as its components."[2] EAD is a system of encoding web pages to provide additional metadata and better description for finding aids. It has become a generally accepted standard by which finding aids appear online.

By setting priorities you will learn to organize your work as well as your thoughts. Every day is different, and most of your day will revolve around reference requests and collaborative projects, but you also need to manage your time to allow work on specific projects. Set deadlines for those projects so that you will complete them. Don't be afraid to say no or ask that you get more time to finish a project if you need it. If your supervisor requests that you put up a new exhibit every year or even every month to "keep things fresh," explain to him or her that you have other responsibilities or other projects demanding your time. If your supervisor insists that you take on a new project, ask if you can drop another project or responsibility to make it happen. You may have to demonstrate your workload so that your supervisor understands why you are saying no. It is easy to fall into the trap of taking on myriad unrelated tasks. If these tasks start to overwhelm you, review your job description with your supervisor and make it clear that your time needs to be focused on your archival duties.

Establish goals for yourself from the start. By setting goals you can determine whether or not you made any progress and reference these goals during performance reviews or program reviews as necessary. Your governing body may set goals for you as well. Make sure that the goals are not too ambitious, and, if they are dependent on other people or departments, make sure they are realistic. When working on collaborative projects, set up a meeting with all parties involved in the project to outline your goals and time line, as well as to allocate responsibilities. Employers are often unaware of the complexity of archival work as well as the multiple tasks you manage daily. Departments that depend on you may not always realize the amount of work that goes on behind the scenes that enables you to answer their reference requests.

It is nearly impossible to predict your day outside of scheduled meetings, so plan to make time for larger projects. If you are involved in a larger project:

- Determine whether or not that project is worth your time or within your abilities and scope of work.

- Set aside time each day or week to work on the project to complete it by the specified deadline.

- If it is your own project, set a realistic deadline for yourself so that the project will be completed rather than abandoned.

- Each day, make a list of things that you need to accomplish. This will help you to prioritize your day to complete the necessary tasks and set aside other, less urgent requests or projects until you can give them your full attention.

Renée DesRoberts repairs and inspects microfilm at the McArthur Public Library in Biddeford, Maine. *Photograph courtesy of Renée DesRoberts.*

Creating Policies

To create some order out of chaos, you should create new or evaluate existing policies. In a small shop it is important to put policies in place, not only to define the mission and scope of your collections, but also to simplify your workload. You need to devise policies for researchers and colleagues. These policies should define the who, what, where, and when of archives. Who has access to what, when, and for how long? Where can you find what? When can someone access the archives?

Policies for staff or yourself should include:

- An access policy

- A collections policy

- A "when I'm away" guide

- A records management policy

- A processing guide

Over time, you may find that other policies need to be created in addition to the policies listed above.

Policies regarding use by researchers and other patrons should include an access policy and reading room rules. These policies should define the basic parameters of the archives and provide you with a framework to determine your daily workflow.

Let's take a look at the difference between creating policies for staff versus policies for researchers.

Policies for Staff

Chances are that even if you are alone most of the time, there are other non-archivist staff members, volunteers, or interns who may work with your collections. Creating policies to protect your collections may be a sensitive subject, especially if there has been a long-standing tradition of taking materials from the archives and then sometimes returning them. This is a common practice in smaller organizations with volunteer or part-time archivists tending to the collection. It will take some time for everyone to adjust to a change in policy, and you may need quite a bit of charm and finesse to ensure that its enforcement goes smoothly.

Rather than writing up a policy and expecting that people will immediately comply or even understand your new demands, talk to your supervisor and explain why you would like to change or create policies that address access to the archives. Demonstrate the importance of the archives to the institution and how the items in the collection are unique and cannot be replaced if lost, stolen, or damaged. You should also hold a staff meeting, particularly if you are part of a library and the librarians have access to the archives. It is also important to include volunteers or interns in this discussion if they have access to materials.

If you currently have a circulating collection, review the policy. How and where do the materials circulate? Reduce circulation to specific people or locations by providing forms and sign-out sheets to document who has taken what and when. Keep a tally of who has borrowed what materials and when. Check in periodically to see if that person is finished with the materials. Often that person has forgotten he or she borrowed an item and no longer needs it. Regardless, do not allow unique materials to be "checked out" without a formal procedure to keep track of who borrowed or used the materials last. This includes materials that you pull for researchers or exhibits.

When creating a policy and talking to colleagues, think about how you can provide appropriate access without compromising the collections. Consider making access by appointment only. If there is a need for access outside normal working hours, is there someone that you can trust to provide access to the materials? If someone from your board, the president, or other important stakeholder comes by and asks for something and it is missing because someone "borrowed" or lost the item, this is unfortunate, but it is a good opportunity to demonstrate the importance of restricted access to the collections.

When writing policies, create a system for "borrowing" items from the collection. This doesn't mean items necessarily circulate, but you may need to pull items for an exhibit, for digitizing, or other projects. Purchase "file out" cards, which are available from archival suppliers to mark the spot where you pulled an item. These cards are available in letter and legal sizes and are made of cardboard stock with tabs so that you can easily find where the item is to be returned. Another option is to create a sign-out sheet to put in place of the item that has been pulled. Either option will work, but be sure that you include the following information:

- Who borrowed the item

- When it was lent out

- Where the item is currently located, such as someone's office, a vendor, and so on

Other policies that will allow you to gain control over your collections are a records management policy for internal records (if applicable) and policies dictating how to handle researchers in your absence. (See Chapter 4 for more information about records management policies and programs.)

It is important, however, to have a policy in place for your colleagues in the event that they wish to use the archives when you are away. You may choose to close the archives during times you are not available. In theory, that is the best policy, however, it is entirely possible that the president, board, or someone else in your organization will have a need for a particular document, photograph, or fact verified when you are away. If possible, assign a trustworthy person to fill this role. Draft a manual for that person that describes where things are, how to find them, how to handle items, and how to sign out materials, if necessary. Make sure that the manual stresses that the archives should only be accessed for important requests, not for casual requests or requests that can wait until you return. An important request could be classified as something with a deadline that cannot wait for your return, such as verification of a particular date so that members of the city council can vote at their next meeting. A request that can wait would be from a researcher planning a visit to your archives to spend the day reviewing documents related to research or someone asking a question out of curiosity.

Policies for Researchers

Your policies for researchers will be different from the policies you establish for your colleagues. Consider your audience. Are you serving as an archive for your institution with no public access, are you serving only students or faculty, or are you serving everyone from staff to the public? This will determine what policies you adopt and how you enforce them.

One of the first steps you should take is to establish an access policy.[3] This policy will define the hours for you and for the researcher. Your work schedule will most likely be dictated by your institution, but you can establish reading room hours that are within your work hours. If you are by yourself, you should consider making your availability to researchers by appointment only. If you only serve an internal constituency, then your normal working hours will be your hours and your "researchers" will be served as they make their requests. Another option is to allow open hours within your normal workday, such as 10 a.m. to 12 noon and then 1 to 4 p.m. No matter what hours you establish, expect to be contacted by both staff and researchers at any time during normal business hours. It is up to you to enforce your own access policy.

The access policy should also define *who* can access the collections. This will depend greatly on your institution. The institution's mission statement will most likely define your patron base. If you are a historical society, you are likely to be open to anyone, but if you are a corporate archives, you may only permit employees of the company to use the archives. Most important, your access policy should follow any and all applicable federal, state, and local laws, as well as any institutional policies regarding who will have access to specific materials in the collections.

Now that your researchers, whether internal or external, know when they can access the archives, you need to decide where they can use the materials. Do you have a reading room or a table for researchers to consult materials? There is no need for anything elaborate, and most likely the area or table you use for processing, receiving, and arranging materials will be the same space you use for your researchers. The space must be kept clear for you and your researchers to be successful in your work.

No matter what kind of space you have, you need to ensure that the area where your researcher is working can accommodate his or her needs and is secure. Make sure that researchers can safely view the materials without mixing them with other materials that might be lying around. Create an easy sight line between you and the researcher to ensure the safety of the collections as well as yourself. If you cannot easily see the researcher from where you are working, make time to check in with the researcher periodically.

Be sure to address where you stand on bags, coats, cameras, computers, and other items people might bring in. You may want to restrict researchers from having easy access to their bags or coats, as it would be easy to slip a document into a pocket. This, however, may be a challenge if your space is not conducive to storing and securing bags or coats away from the research area. If this is the case, request that patrons keep their bags and coats at their feet and under the table rather than next to them so that you will be able to hear or see them if they reach for the bag. You may also need to make an exception and allow researchers to keep coats with them if the area where they are working is cold.

If you have audiovisual materials, microfilm, or microfiche, provide equipment for playing or viewing those items. If you do not, notify your researchers that those collections are not accessible. There may be cases where some materials need to be restricted to preserve the items. Excessive handling of fragile or damaged items can cause irreparable damage.

To protect the materials further, you should put policies in place to restrict practices that could cause damage. You should establish a "no food and drinks" rule to protect the items from both spillage and the potential for attracting insects that could destroy your collections. Asking researchers to not bring

FIGURE 1   **SUFFOLK UNIVERSITY ARCHIVES**
            READING ROOM POLICIES AND PROCEDURES

Welcome to the Suffolk University Archives. This facility is open to students, staff, faculty and the general public. In order to provide you with quality service, we have established the following procedures:

1. Read the Reading Room Policy and complete a **Reading Room Registration Form** on your first visit to the collection in any given academic year.

2. Materials in the Moakley Archive **do not circulate**, and may be used only in the Reading Room.

3. If you plan to use a large collection or a large amount of materials, we appreciate advance notice to prepare for your visit.

4. **No food or drink allowed** in the Reading Room.

5. Lockers and locks are provided for personal items. You may take a notebook (bound or spiral); paper for note-taking is available from Archives staff.

6. Laptop computers may be used in the Reading Room. Please leave the carrying case in a locker.

7. **Please turn off all cell phones and pagers.**

8. Cameras, scanners and other photo duplication devices are not allowed.

9. Please wash your hands before you handle any archival material or supplies and after any food breaks.

10. **Use pencil only!** Pen ink can damage collection materials. Pencils are available in the Reading Room.

11. **Handle materials with care.** Please do not exert pressure on the materials, such as leaning on, tracing, or writing on them. Gloves for handling photographs and fragile items are available from Archives staff.

12. **Please retain the order in which manuscript and photograph collections are placed in the boxes and folders. Use "Place Markers" when removing folders or files from a box, and please remove only one folder or file at a time.**

13. If you would like photocopies, please consult with a staff member. Reasonable requests can be accommodated depending on the condition of the materials and staffing levels.

14. Members of the Suffolk University community will receive 20 courtesy copies free of charge.

15. Please be aware that retrieval for off-site material may take 2–3 days.

Courtesy of the Suffolk University Archives

bags into the archives will help to reduce theft. Researchers should only be allowed to use pencil so that they cannot make marks on your materials with ink.

Figure 1 is a good example of reading room policies and procedures from Suffolk University. Outlining and posting rules for researchers is an important step to help researchers understand what to expect when using your archives. Because most researchers often begin their research online, it is a good idea to post these rules and policies on your website.

Conclusion

Walking into a small repository, whether you are its first archivist or its tenth, is no easy feat. You need to review what the previous archivist(s) has done and either start from scratch or refine the existing situation. As the sole archivist, you need to learn to manage not only your collections but yourself. Get yourself organized by creating policies, but writing policies is only the first step. Have your governing body approve those policies and enforce them.

When working alone, it is important to keep in mind that although you should do your best, don't get hung up on perfection. It is easy to become overwhelmed by all of the work that may come your way, but it is essential that you learn to take things in stride; learn to say no while trying your best to meet the demands of your job. Your task is to carry out a full range of responsibilities by keeping several activities going simultaneously. Make the most of it, because this is one of life's great opportunities!

NOTES

[1] See Appendix A for publication information.

[2] Richard Pearce-Moses, *A Glossary of Archival and Records Terminology* (Chicago: Society of American Archivists, 2005), available at http://www.archivists.org/glossary/.

[3] For more information on access policies, see Mary Jo Pugh, *Providing Reference Services for Archives and Manuscripts* (Chicago: Society of American Archivists, 2005).

THE LONE ARRANGER IN A LOCAL GOVERNMENT ARCHIVES SETTING

BY JOHN H. SLATE

Established in 1985, the Dallas Municipal Archives is a part of the City Secretary's Office of the City of Dallas and is a repository for the historic and permanently valuable records of city government. Its mission is to document and preserve the actions of the City of Dallas and to effectively provide public access to information. The archives serves to help citizens and city employees research city history, such as the history of a neighborhood, a historic election, or events in the city's past in a variety of ways.

While some local government archives programs are created without legislation or authority, the Dallas Municipal Archives is somewhat unique because it exists by legal mandate. Chapter 39C, the City of Dallas records management ordinance, states that the archives, as a part of the records management program, "serves as the repository for permanent and historical city records that are transferred to the facility by departments." Further strengthening the archives' goals are portions of the same ordinance, explicitly charging the records management program and all of its agents to protect the essential records of the city and properly preserve city records that are of historical value.

A government archives is similar to a corporate archives in the sense that it serves its internal users just as much, if not more, than its external users. Because of the nature of government records, the research value is sometimes perceived as less useful to the public as it is to employees of government. However, the only limit on the use of government archives to any researcher, external or internal, is creativity and industry in research.

The most salient feature of a government records archives program, and one with major impact for a lone arranger, is the inherent high level of organization. Because there is rarely overlap from one department to another, the filing units are usually—but not always—defined by its parent department. This allows the archivist to spend less time determining the hierarchy and more time determining whether or not the records are permanent.

Being part of an entity with a formal records management program is one of the greatest benefits to the government records lone arranger. Without this mechanism, archivists are often forced to spend more time identifying records for acquisition than should be necessary. In a city government like Dallas, Texas, there is a robust records management program that aggressively works with each department to help identify, store, retrieve, and schedule for disposition approximately 84,000 cubic feet of records. Because only about 1 percent of those records will ever become permanent, it is incumbent on the archivist and records manager to stay aware of what has permanent and enduring value. Although there are certain classes of records value that will automatically become permanent by law, communicating the interests of the archives to records management can yield significant rewards.

The ordered, scheduled records in a records management program frequently, though not always, can arrive at an archives as a result of an "authorization for destruction" order. In an ideal relationship with the records management operation, the archivist should be notified when records are slated for destruction to allow for a final appraisal for possible evidential, historical, and even intrinsic value. Age, comprehensiveness, and information that contributes to an understanding of decision making in a local government can appear in records that seemingly have no further value.

Nothing, however, beats one's familiarity with a local government's internal structure, its departments, and the key contacts in those departments. Anticipating events such as retirements, mass turnovers in staffing, anniversaries, and departmental consolidations can have very important benefits to the lone arranger. Never forsake the moment one hears the words, "there's a closet over there I haven't looked in for years."

Being a one-person archival program in a local government records setting can be either a blessing or a curse. Without a staff, there are fewer personnel issues and no time spent on time reporting. However, this also means the burden is borne fully on the archivist's shoulders. Conducting all aspects of work means that prioritization is critical to any level of success. In creating a schedule for processing, it is important to anticipate user needs and identify collections having immediate and timely use. The records of a local government's administration, such as a charter, civil and criminal codes, annual reports, and budgets, are vital tools that may be requested at any time and should be considered above collections with more esoteric interest.

There are always matters that cannot be controlled, such as funding, and appropriate adjustments are necessary. Exhibits and public events can be cut back; opening hours can be reduced, but not the basic functions that constitute a formal archives program. Acquisition, arrangement and description, preservation, and reference all must continue in some form. Outreach can be performed at minimal cost, such as speaking before groups, writing articles, and participating in public events where the archives' name can be displayed. National History Day, historic commemorations, Archives Month, and even the occasional "Archives Road Show" can attract attention and good publicity for your institution without great expense.

Lone arrangers often comment, "I never have time to process collections." Volunteers and interns are an invaluable part of a lone arranger's arsenal in the battle against processing backlogs. With careful instruction, many basic tasks such as writing preliminary checklists and rough inventories can be assigned to volunteers. It is important to identify good working skills and mature independent workers early, because archivists are not baby-sitters. Undergraduate or graduate-level students are ideal volunteers or interns, especially ones in public history or archives programs, who are often motivated. Volunteers with good writing skills can be extremely helpful in the creation of descriptive notes and other information. The drawback to interns is that their time is limited, and once their coursework is complete, they are out the door.

There are tradeoffs for being a lone arranger in a local government archives, but the rewards are invaluable. The respect of your coworkers and the government's administration and, perhaps most importantly, the satisfaction in knowing that you have used public tax dollars to do something lasting and permanent that can have social benefit is something that offsets the less wonderful aspects of working inside a government.

"What Is This Stuff?"
Collections Management

In *A Glossary of Archival and Records Terminology*, Richard Pearce-Moses defines **accession**: "Materials physically and legally transferred to a repository as a unit at a single time; an acquisition," or "to take legal and physical custody of a group of records or other materials and to formally document their receipt." It also means "to document the transfer of records or materials in a register, database, or other log of the repository's holdings."

The materials may be acquired by gift, bequest, purchase, transfer, retention schedule, or statute. An accession may be part of a larger, existing collection. An accession added to existing collections is sometimes called an accretion or an accrual.

"Accession" should be distinguished from "acquisition." As nouns, they are synonymous. However, the verb "accession" goes far beyond the sense of "acquire," connoting the initial steps of processing by establishing rudimentary physical and intellectual control over the materials by entering brief information about those materials in a register, database, or other log of the repository's holdings.[2]

The bulk of an archivist's job lies in collections management. This task generally takes up more than half of your time—more, if you are starting an archive. Managing collections includes acquiring (through internal acquisitions, gifts, or by purchasing), accessioning, arranging, describing, and organizing. Often archivists in small shops have large backlogs and may have minimal information about what a collection contains, where it came from, and how it is arranged. Getting a handle on these records will make life easier when someone requests the materials or uses materials for reference or you need to do an exhibit.

Acquisitions

Acquisitions at your institution will depend on a number of factors, but most importantly it should be based on a clearly defined collections policy. Your collections policy is the determining factor for what you acquire and discard.

When defining your collecting scope, the best place to start is by creating a collections policy. A collections policy should follow the mission of your institution (or archives) while providing the scope of your collections and defining your conditions for accepting gifts and donations. By creating a policy, you can determine what types of materials will make up the core of your collections; this will provide you with a set of guidelines that enables you to accept, turn away, or deaccession collections.

First, you will need to craft your mission statement, if you don't already have one. It should be the opening statement of your collections policy, and if you have a website, it should be displayed on your homepage. If you are part of a library, your mission statement may be determined for you, but your collections policy should still include a mission statement specifically for the archives. This policy should answer these questions:

- What activities, groups, or experiences does the archives document?
- Why was the archives started?
- What does the archives collect?
- What groups does the archives serve?[1]

Figures 1–3 are examples of mission statements representing various types of institutions as well as diverse formats.

. . . .

FIGURE 1   DIOCESE OF WILMINGTON ARCHIVES

The Archives of the Diocese of Wilmington, an activity of the Chancery Office within the Department of Pastoral Services, will (1) identify and preserve the non-current records of enduring value originated by offices and activities of the Diocese of Wilmington, and on a selective basis, those originated by its parishes, together with other papers and selected artifacts pertaining to the Diocese, and (2) provide for their use for administrative, legal and historical purposes. The Archives is the historical archive of the diocese mandated by Canon 491 Section 2, but does not replace or substitute for individual parish archives mandated by Canon 535 Section 4.

The mission of the archives, as with any work of the Diocese, relates to the saving work of Christ, documenting its impact on the people of God within the particular Church of Wilmington. By allowing us to know what happened in the past, the Archives helps us recognize the demands of grace in the present and prepare for what it will ask of us in the future. Archives activities are not merely a remembrance of the past, but a work of faith for the present and the future.

Courtesy of the Diocese of Wilmington Archives, Wilmington, Delaware

. . . .
. . . .

FIGURE 2   ALBUQUERQUE ACADEMY ARCHIVES

To provide adequate facilities for the retention, preservation, servicing and research use of such records.

To serve as a research center for the study of the Academy's history by members of the Academy and the scholarly community at large.

To provide reference services to assist in the Academy's administration and operations.

To serve in a public relations capacity by promoting knowledge and understanding of the origins, programs and goals of the Academy, and their development.

To facilitate the efficient management of the recorded information produced by the Academy's departments and offices.

Courtesy of the Albuquerque Academy Archives, Albuquerque, New Mexico

. . . .
. . . .

FIGURE 3   SANTA ANA HISTORY ROOM

Santa Ana History Room is committed to fostering an interest in local history by collecting, preserving and making available materials of enduring historical value relating to the development of the City of Santa Ana and Orange County.

Courtesy of the Santa Ana History Room, Santa Ana Public Library, Santa Ana, California

. . . .

{ KEY TERMS

Deaccessioning: "The process by which an archives, museum, or library permanently removes accessioned materials from its holdings. Deaccessioned material may be offered back to its donor, offered to another institution, or destroyed." Another term for deaccessioning is *permanent withdrawal*.[3]

When crafting a collections policy, consider your audience. In most cases you will need to revise the policy multiple times to appease your constituency. Be sure that they understand the purpose of the policy by explaining why you have included particular clauses, but keep in mind that you need to be word-savvy in order to achieve your goals. You must also examine the availability of institutional resources. Will the policy generate too many records? As a responsible archivist, you don't want to overcommit to the point that your archives cannot accept further donations or records.

A well-crafted policy should include the following elements:

- A statement of purpose
- Clientele served by the archives
- Priorities of the collection
- Items or subject material not collected
- A statement regarding your deaccessioning practices or policies
- Any cooperative agreements (such as shared collections or facilities with other archives)
- Statements related to resource sharing
- Statements concerning gift acceptance or refusal

To keep your policy in line with your collecting goals and resources, and to validate it and secure a commitment from your institution, have your institution's governing body review and approve the policy every few years. Figure 4 is the collections policy from the National Press Club Archives. It incorporates the major elements of a well-rounded policy and was approved by the Club's Board of Governors in 2004.

Once you have a collections policy that satisfies all interested parties, you can begin working on your daily operating policies and procedures. These include:

- Deed of gift forms
- Accession forms
- Researcher guidelines (including internal researchers)
- Researcher sign-in sheets and/or reference request forms
- Pricing schedules, if applicable

Not all of these forms are necessary. Only you can determine their necessity based on your daily operations. For example, if you accept only internal records, then you will not need a deed of gift form, but you should create an accessions form that will give you the necessary information about the records that come to you on a regular or not-so-regular basis. Whether you use an accessions form or a deed of gift, you need to have some control over what

When crafting a collections policy, consider your audience.

FIGURE 4   THE NATIONAL PRESS CLUB ARCHIVES

Purpose

The National Press Club Archives collects, preserves, describes, exhibits and makes available to researchers materials related to the history and activities of the National Press Club and the history of journalism, specifically in the Washington, D.C. area.

Scope of Materials

The following are materials collected by the National Press Club Archives:

- Materials in any format concerning National Press Club affairs, including social events, news events, professional affairs and administrative activities.

- Materials in any format concerning the Women's National Press Club/ Washington Press Club affairs, including social events, news events, professional affairs and administrative activities.

- Administrative records, including paper, photographs, audio and video tapes and other related materials of professional associations in journalism or public relations. These associations are for the professional development and socialization of groups in journalism or public relations. These associations should either be national in scope or based in the Washington, D.C. area.

- Personal papers and related material concerning the National Press Club, including photographs, belonging to Silver Owls or Golden Owls of the National Press Club (25-year or 50-year Club members).

- Personal papers and related material in any format belonging to winners of the National Press Club's Fourth Estate Award.

- Personal papers of journalists who have spent a significant portion of their careers covering events in Washington, D.C.

- Published biographies about journalists, publishers, broadcasters, producers and other notables in the media industry, printed at least forty years prior to the date of accession into the Archives. Modern reprints will not be accepted into the Archives.

- Published autobiographies and memoirs of journalists, publishers and other notables in the media industry, with a concentration on books printed at least forty years prior to the date of accession into the Archives. Modern reprints will not be accepted into the Archives.

- Published books on the history of Washington, D.C., including memoirs of Washington, D.C. residents highlighting the city and its environs, published before 1975.

(cont.)

(Figure 4 cont.)

- Original editorial cartoons of any date (photocopies or newspaper/magazine clippings of cartoons will not be accepted).

Gifts Policy

The National Press Club Archives is happy to accept donations that fall within the scope of its collection policy. Any collection accepted commits us to the task of organizing and preserving it, which involves hand labor and costs for archival supplies. Donors are encouraged to include a monetary donation to fund the cost of processing and preserving their materials. Due to limited staffing, budget and space, all donations or gifts are subject to review by the National Press Club Archives and may be declined. Partial collections are discouraged but may be reviewed at the discretion of the Archives. The National Press Club Archives reserves the right to decline any collection for the following reasons:

- Inability of the National Press Club Archives to provide suitable space, staffing, supplies and equipment. While the lack of one or more of these does not constitute a compelling reason for refusing archives and manuscripts, deficiency in one or more may constitute grounds for a temporary delay in their acquisition. During periods of severe deficiency in any of these areas, the archives will give priority to new accessions of internal records whenever possible.

- Inability of the National Press Club Archives to provide sufficient support to preserve and provide access to archival records.

- The collection contains materials that do not fit within the scope of the National Press Club Archives.

- Materials that can be found in other archives or libraries will not be accepted (ex. newspapers, books, published and unpublished ephemera).

- Photocopies of materials donated to another repository will not be accepted.

- Materials irreparably damaged or infested by insects or mold will not be accepted.

- Materials in which the donor's ownership is in question or is disputed will not be accepted.

- Duplicate materials will not be accepted due to lack of space and may be subject to disposal.

- The National Press Club Archives will not accept permanent loans of materials and will not assume liability for materials that are not owned by the National Press Club.

Once a donation is accepted, a deed of gift must be signed by the donor specifying the materials to be donated. This deed of gift transfers any rights the donor may have concerning ownership or copyright to the National Press Club Archives. Special conditions may be specified by the donor, but the National Press Club Archives may refuse any donation in which it deems the conditions of use are overly restrictive.

Donors are welcome to examine the material that they have donated at any time, and, if so desired, can be given a copy of any inventories, finding aids, or other research materials produced by the Archives about the donated material.

The National Press Club Archives is a nonprofit organization and has been granted 501 (c) (3) tax-exempt status by the IRS. Donations may qualify as tax-deductible. This, however, does not permit the archivist to appraise gifts. Under IRS regulations no library, archive, or museum can perform an appraisal. The National Press Club Archives will not hire an independent appraiser. If you would like your collection appraised for tax purposes, please arrange for this to happen before you donate your collection to the National Press Club Archives.

Cooperative Collection Development Efforts

The National Press Club Archives will work with other institutions involved in similar efforts, as appropriate.

Courtesy of the National Press Club Archives, Washington, D.C.

Establishing control over your collection is essential to the success of your institution.

comes into the archives. You can find examples of these forms online or in *Sample Forms for Archival & Records Management Programs*, published by the Society of American Archivists (SAA) and ARMA International (see Appendix A for more information on this book).

Establishing control over your collection is essential to the success of your institution. Once you have your policies in place, it is time to implement them. Survey your collections and determine what fits into your collecting scope and what does not belong. One thing to consider is how the material was acquired. If there is something that doesn't quite fit or doesn't fit at all, try to determine how it arrived in your archives. Is it a book signed by the founder of your organization or his or her relative? Was it something donated by someone on your executive board? Is it a collection that has been revered or mentioned in any previous publications by your organization? Look for a deed of gift, correspondence, or other agreement before determining whether or not the item should be deaccessioned. Not all previously acquired collections that don't fit under your new collections policy should be deaccessioned.

There may be some collections that you need to keep for political reasons more than practical reasons. If the collection or even individual items cause potential problems because they are in poor physical condition or have mold or insects, then you need to negotiate the fate of those materials. If something doesn't fit but is considered "important" and needs conservation treatment, you should petition for the necessary funds to do so.

After determining which collections you would like to deaccession, you need to decide what to do with those materials. Anything that has been infested with insects or mold should be discarded. Before discarding any other materials, even if they are in poor condition, consider whether or not it may be useful to another institution. For example, if your institution is in Kansas but you have materials relating to a county in New Jersey, you may want to offer it to an institution in that location. Many institutions offer materials through e-mail distribution lists such as the Archives and Archivists listserv maintained by the SAA.

Once you have defined the core of your collection, you need to take a look at your next steps. This is where the questions—What is your directive? and Who is your audience?—come into play and your mission statement becomes important. If your purpose is simply to serve your organization and not the general public, then your mission will be much different from that of an archivist whose main constituency is the general public. Craft your policies based on your charge. Is it more important to create a researcher policy, or is it more beneficial to create an accessions form?

Managing Acquisitions

When acquiring materials from outside the institution, you need to establish whether or not you have a budget for purchasing materials or if all of your acquisitions will be donations or gifts. If your institution does not acquire materials from outside, you will need to establish a records management program (see Chapter 4). If you acquire materials both internally and externally, you will need a records management program, a donation policy, and a deed of gift form. Smaller institutions often do not have a budget for acquisitions, so it is common to acquire all materials on a rolling basis through donations or a records management program.

On rare occasions, you may find yourself taking a field trip to assess a collection for possible acquisition. If you do not have the resources, such as a vehicle, time outside of your work hours, or compensation from your institution, you may not be able to assess and acquire collections off-site unless you do so on your own time. Many small institutions will not support travel for appraisal and acquisition of materials. Let donors know your limitations and ask them to come to you if at all possible. Otherwise you may have to decline their offers.

Deeds of Gift

Once you have determined how you will acquire materials, you will need a deed of gift form. The deed of gift form should include:

- The name of the donor

- The date

- The scope and content of the donation

- Any copyright, trademark, or other intellectual property rights issues

- Language in the form stating that the material being donated is the property of the donor

- A check box and options for what the donor would like the archivist to do with any materials that are not kept

- The donors' signature and your signature

Figure 5 is from the Jewish Buffalo Archives Project and represents a well-thought-out deed of gift that can be used by many types of institutions. This form contains all of the key components needed for a legally sound deed of gift.

In contrast to the well-developed policy of the Jewish Buffalo Archives Project, the deed of gift formerly used by the Montgomery County Historical Society in Rockville, Maryland, is poorly constructed and would not stand up in court if a dispute were to arise in relation to these materials (see Figure 6).

If your institution has a development office or a legal department, consult with them on what should be included in your deed of gift. Some institutions may require that the deeds be written on a case-by-case basis or that a general deed of gift be used only for smaller, less valuable (in monetary terms) collections.

Deeds of gift should be kept together in a clearly marked file drawer or box. If you keep your deeds of gift electronically, keep them in one file and make sure they remain accessible. You probably won't be the last person in charge of the archives, and it is important to maintain a record of the origination of items in your archives. Keeping records prevents someone from coming forward to reclaim that collection. By documenting your collections, you have something on paper to show that a person donated materials to your institution in good faith; in the case of any dispute, the law will determine who has legal ownership.

Another reason to have a deed of gift is to document when the collection was acquired and whether or not items within the collection can be disposed of and how. It should be clear how those items should be discarded. Can they be offered to other institutions or thrown away, or has the donor requested that the materials be returned to him or her? Donors may want to add stipulations on whether or not you can sell items in the collection or if they want any deaccessioned items to be offered to specific institutions.

FIGURE 5 **BUREAU OF JEWISH EDUCATION OF GREATER BUFFALO**
JEWISH BUFFALO ARCHIVES PROJECT

805 Delaware Avenue

Buffalo, New York 14209

DEED OF GIFT

The Jewish Buffalo Archives Project, Bureau of Jewish Education of Greater Buffalo, gratefully acknowledges the gift of the archival material described below,

Name of Institution/ Individual/Group	Address	Telephone / E-mail
Date	Accession Number(s)	
Donor	Street	City/State/ZIP
Contact Person	Telephone / E-mail	

The donation described below has been received by the Jewish Buffalo Archives Project/Bureau of Jewish Education as a gift, and the owner or his agent with full authority, desiring to absolutely transfer full title by signing below, hereby gives, assigns, and conveys finally and completely, and without any limitation or reservation, the property described below to the Jewish Buffalo Archives Project/Bureau of Jewish Education of Greater Buffalo and assigns permanently and forever, together with (when applicable) any copyrights therein and the right to copyright the same. This material will be made accessible by the Jewish Buffalo Archives Project/Bureau of Jewish Education, through its partner the University Archives at State University of New York at Buffalo (University at Buffalo).
Description of Donation
Credit Line (How you would like your organization to be acknowledged)
* It is my preference that any items which the Archives Project decides not to retain shall be: ____ Returned to Donor ____ Destroyed ____ Other (Specify) _____
By my signature below I accept the foregoing conditions and acknowledge reading "The Conditions Governing Gifts" below.
Signatures Donor _____ Date _____ Printed Name _____ Archivist _____ Date _____

The Conditions Governing Gifts

1. It is understood that all gifts are outright and unconditional unless otherwise noted upon this gift agreement. The donor relinquishes whatever physical and intellectual property rights s/he possesses to the contents.

2. Gifts to the Archives may be deductible in accordance with provisions of federal income tax laws.

3. The donor named on this form has not received any goods or services from the Archives in return for this gift.

4. The Archivist is not permitted to furnish appraisals.

5. The Archives gratefully acknowledges your gift and wishes to thank you for this valued addition to the historical collections of the Jewish Community Archives.

6. Please indicate on the form beside "CREDIT LINE" how you would like to be acknowledged in any news releases or other publicity regarding this donation.

7. It is understood and agreed that the materials donated shall become the exclusive and absolute property of the Jewish Buffalo Archives Project/ Bureau of Jewish Education. This property will be handled according to the procedures established in the Jewish Buffalo Archives Project Collections Management policy.

8. All access to the gifted material shall be at the sole discretion of University Archives of State University of New York at Buffalo (University at Buffalo). Information and policies are subject to change. For the latest, see: http://library.buffalo.edu/specialcollections/about/.

(Revision January 30, 2009).

Courtesy of the Jewish Buffalo Archives Project, Buffalo, New York

Internal Acquisitions

Internal acquisitions can be just as challenging as external acquisitions. If you have a well-defined records management policy in place and all departments know which records should be turned over to the archives, you are well ahead of most lone arrangers. Archivists who do not have a records management program in place often find themselves educating staff about what should be kept and what should be thrown away. Internal staff members rarely understand what an archivist does—other than collect old stuff.

Because of this lack of knowledge, archivists often find themselves with "dump and run" acquisitions. These are materials that just show up on the doorstep with an occasional note saying who dropped off the materials or some other pertinent information. This happens with both internal and external donations; however, you can usually track down the culprit if the materials came from an

FIGURE 6   DEED OF GIFT FORM

Deed of Gift

MCHS

MONTGOMERY
C O U N T Y
HISTORICAL
S O C I E T Y

tel (301) 340-2825

fax (301) 340-2871

111

West

Montgomery

Avenue

Rockville

Maryland

20850-4212

Date: _____

The following gift(s) is/are made to the Montgomery County Historical Society with no limiting conditions and in full knowledge that complete title of owner-ship—including the right to determine owner of the object(s), and that to the best of my knowledge, all right, title and interests are mine to give.

Description of object(s):

_____   _____
Signature of donor   Signature for MCHS

_____   _____
Name of donor   Name of MCHS staff

_____   _____
Address of donor   Title

_____
Phone

_____
Email

www.montgomeryhistory.org

Courtesy of the Montgomery County Historical Society, Rockville, MD internal source. To prevent "dump and run" acquisitions, educate your staff about what to keep, and create transfer guidelines for offices to follow. These guidelines should tell departments how to box and prepare materials, how to create an inventory list, how to fill out any transfer forms, and how to get the materials to you safely. If you can, develop a records management program (see Chapter 4 for more details). Figure 7 provides guidance to internal offices on how to properly transfer material to the archives and hopefully prevent "dump and runs."

Documenting New Acquisitions

You need a plan to handle incoming collections, both in terms of physical space and documentation. Your physical space may determine what and how much material you can acquire. If your institution requires you to take material and you don't have the space, it is important that you bring this to the attention of your supervisor or executive board. You may have to store materials in less-than-ideal conditions and in multiple locations until you can establish a more suitable space. (Planning and preparing for improvements and expansion of physical space will be discussed in Chapter 5.)

Set aside a space where you can place newly acquired materials until you can properly assess and accession the items. This may be a challenge. Often you won't have any space to do this, or you may need to use your researcher area as a multipurpose area to accession new materials, process collections, and serve researchers. You can make it work by staying on top of your new acquisitions and trying to identify and integrate these materials into your collections as quickly as possible.

Part of this process requires that you assess the materials for any preservation issues, particularly issues that may adversely affect your current collections. Mold, insects, and rodents are major hazards to you and your collections. *Do not* mix new materials with current materials until you have at least opened each box to know what is inside. If you do not detect any immediate threat, set the materials aside until you can do a more thorough check. Mold may only appear in small areas and you can easily miss it; if your storage area has the ideal conditions for mold growth, you may end up with a larger problem than you anticipated. (See Chapters 4 and 5 for discussions of managing mold and insects.)

Once you have established where you will store new materials, you need to put in place a system to deal with those acquisitions. Gaining control of new collections starts with your deed of gift, but it does not end there. Documenting new acquisitions is important to the appraisal process. Consider keeping control files, or files that contain materials such as any box lists, correspondence, photographs, or other materials related to the collection that are not part of the collection. More importantly, number these collections. You should start a system of numbering new acquisitions and place that number on the boxes

Gaining control of new collections starts with your deed of gift, but it does not end there.

FIGURE 7 **EMERSON COLLEGE ARCHIVES**
ARCHIVAL MATERIAL TRANSFER GUIDELINES

These procedures are designed to minimize physical deterioration or damage to records transferred to the Archives and to ensure that they will be readily retrievable after transfer.

1. Consult your departments' record schedule and/or the Archivist to determine what materials should be sent to the archives. Materials sent to archives that are determined to have no long-term archival value will be returned.

2. Conduct a Records Survey to identify and separate active records from archival materials.

3. Shred any copies of materials that were created by another department but used for administrative purposes in your department. The archives will receive the original documents from the originating department.

4. Obtain Record Storage boxes for your records. Boxes can be ordered from Hollinger Metal Edge (item RSB-12, Record Storage Box White Acid-Free Corrugated Board).

5. Remove all hanging file folders. If items are loose within a hanging file folder, place them into a regular office file and transfer the name of the file from the hanging file to the new file using pencil. Please print legibly.

6. Fill boxes (from front to back) with files; maintain the order in which the files were created or used and do not over-pack the box.

7. Label and number the boxes consecutively and discretely in pencil (e.g., [Name of Department], Date, Box 1 of 7). Do not use pen or apply labels to the boxes.

8. Make a list of box contents/inventory (include dates whenever possible).

9. Complete the Records Transfer Form (attach your inventory to the Records Transfer Form).

10. Insert the Records Transfer Form and inventory in the first box; keep a copy for your records.

11. Please do not tape box lids shut.

12. Contact the College Archives in advance of delivery so we know the boxes are coming.

13. Put in a work order to arrange delivery to the College Archives, room 223, 2nd floor of the Walker Building. Please do not leave archival materials outside in the hallway.

14. Upon delivery, notification will be sent to the originating office and a copy of the Records Transfer Form will be returned with an accession number for future retrieval.

Courtesy of the Emerson College Archives, Boston, Massachusetts or other physical containers in pencil on the collections themselves, the deed of gift, and any files related to the collection. This number will help you and anyone else looking at this collection to determine a collection's contents, how they were acquired, and why.

Use any numbering scheme you like for accession or acquisition numbers; however, the generally accepted system of numbering is to write the year first followed by the number of the collection for that year. For example, if you just acquired your fourth collection for 2012, the number may be 2012.04 or 12-04. The zero in front of the number 4 is a placeholder, because you may take in more than nine collections a year, which is quite possible. If you acquire at a rapid rate, you may consider adding two zeros in front of your single-digit numbers as place holders.

Aside from the numbering scheme, it is important to have a system of tracking these numbers either on paper or electronically. This is different from keeping files about a new collection. Whether you operate on paper or electronically, you should keep one file or book that lists the following information:

- Accession number

- Who donated the collection

- When it was acquired

- The amount of materials acquired (e.g., number of boxes or items, linear feet, etc.)

- Whether or not the collection should be retained for a limited amount of time or permanently

If you work primarily on paper, you may want to purchase a ledger book in which you can write each new acquisition and refer to it as needed. If you prefer tracking and keeping files electronically, you have several options. There are also several software options that include an acquisition database as part of the overall management tool.[4] If you don't have a specialized software program for managing your archives, you may want to use something simple like Microsoft Excel or other spreadsheet software that may already exist on your computer. One final option is to create your own database in a program such as Microsoft Access or another software system. Any of these options will help you gain control over your acquisitions.

Organization of Materials

Part of the acquisitions process includes identifying the type of materials that you have in your collection and how these new materials fit in. Archival collections are organized in a hierarchical system due to their physical nature. One way to organize and integrate these materials is by creating group numbers. Because archival collections are not integrated and comingled like library collections, numbering groups of records allows you to acquire materials and add them to the end of an existing group of records. For example, you may have a few boxes of records from the current president of your organization, but because the organization has had more than one president, you may also have several boxes from past presidents in the archives. To identify them all as "records of the president," give them one overall number. This number will be different from the accession number that you assigned to the group of records that came in all at the same time.

By creating a numbering scheme for identifying large groups within the archives, you can also distinguish between your institutional records or those created in the course of your organization's business from any special collections or outside collections you may acquire. To distinguish between internal and external records, consider using two numbering schemes. For example, internal records may be referred to as *record groups*, indicating their function as documentation of your organization. Each department, office, or group within your organization should have a number, and you can break down that system further by adding a decimal point to delineate subgroups. Numbering for internal records may look something like this: RG01—Records of the President; RG01.01—George Washington; RG01.02—John Adams.

KEY TERMS }

Manuscripts or **special collections** are terms often used to describe materials that are generated outside of your organization and contain materials of all formats. These collections can be generated by an individual, family, or organization not affiliated with your institution.

For external groups of records or collections acquired from people or entities outside your organization, you may designate *manuscript* numbers or *special collection* numbers. These numbering schemes are arbitrary; however, for your record groups you may consider numbering groups according to their importance within the institution. For example, you might number your president's records as RG 01. You can number your special collections based on when the items were acquired and numbered; examples include MSS 01 or Sp.Coll. 01.

These numbering schemes are not set in stone and can consist of any combination of abbreviations and numbers that makes the most sense for your institution. What is most important is to have a system that allows you to identify larger groups of records so that you can easily determine which records belong together even if they aren't physically stored together. Whatever scheme you use, make sure that the boxes are clearly labeled. Labels don't need to be fancy; you can simply write them on the box, in pencil and legibly.

In some cases, you may inherit a numbering scheme that does not work for you or is impractical. If very little has been done under this scheme, it may be easy to go back and restructure or renumber items. However, if your entire collection has been numbered under this scheme, you will have to consider whether or not it is worth the time and effort to revise or start over. If the collection was numbered at the item level, that system will have to go! It is not possible to keep up with numbering every individual item. Leave what has already been done and start working on the big picture by defining groups of records rather than individual records. You may find that three-dimensional objects can more easily be defined or described at the item level, but these should still be grouped with their original set of records *if* they are not stand-alone items. That being said, do not force items into a collection if they do not belong together.

Appraisal

For many small institutions, space is at a premium, and some weeding or removing items from your collections is necessary. Appraisal is an important step in determining what is most important and useful to your institution, and you should perform this step with all records whether you acquire them from outside sources or from within. The appraisal process does not require you to place a monetary value on your collections.

Appraisal is the selection of records of enduring value or archival value. These records are defined as those with continuing usefulness or significance based on the administrative, legal, fiscal, evidential, or historical information they contain, justifying their ongoing preservation.[5] When appraising records, consider the following questions:

- Who made the record and for what purpose?

- What is its significance, and how does it document a person, place, or thing?

- Who are the potential users?

- What is the cost of preserving the record versus the benefit of retaining the information?

When looking at internal records, you need to consider the following: the significance of the records creator's position within the organization, the significance of the records, and the significance of the documents' subjects. You should also take into account:

- The uniqueness of the record itself

- The form of the record (Is it in both electronic and paper form, which is the preferred format for long-term preservation?)

- The uniqueness of the information contained in the record

- How scarce the documentation is on this subject

- The ways this record will be useful[6]

Appraisal also means weighing the costs and benefits of acquiring a record. In a small shop, resources are limited, so it may not be feasible to keep records that a larger institution may keep. Conduct a cost benefit analysis when reviewing records. What are the costs and benefits of identifying, appraising, and accessioning records; processing the collections; and preserving the records?[7] Never keep records on a "just in case" basis; you need a clearly defined reason to keep records.

{ KEY TERMS

Appraisal is "The process of identifying materials offered to an archives that have sufficient value to be accessioned" or "The process of determining the length of time records should be retained, based on legal requirements and on their current and potential usefulness."[8]

Appraisal or reappraisal means the opportunity to weed collections and focus them according to your collections policy. Start by looking at the larger picture and identifying whole groups of records that may or may not be relevant to your institution. You don't need to go through them box by box and through every piece of paper unless the records are so disorganized that there is no other way to identify records within a group. Start by trying to find any documentation related to their original acquisition—who donated the materials, when, who accepted the donation, and so on. If you can answer any of these questions, you might have all you need to determine whether or not the records are significant enough to keep. If you cannot answer any of these questions, you may need to look at the collection a bit closer before making your decision.

When choosing collections to deaccession, review your collections policy and ask the following questions:

- Does the collection fit the scope of your current collections policy?

- Can the records be found in another repository?

- Is this collection, or portions of the collection, redundant?

- Does the collection have a deed of gift?

Some collections may have been acquired because the collection and the content may have been unique to its creator. A good example is a collection of newspaper clippings, which may have covered a topic or topics of interest to the collector. If the clippings are not arranged in a usable fashion and come from a large newspaper that has an online archive, this collection no longer serves its purpose and will cost more to preserve than it may be worth.

Another set of records to consider weeding are publications. Keep internal publications, or publications related to your institution; however, you don't need twenty copies. Keep only a few—maybe four at the most—and give away or sell the rest. The same rule applies to duplicates in other collections. You can also weed book collections. If you have a generic collection of books (not related to a specific collection), take a look at the titles to determine if they are of any use to your constituency or if they would be better suited to another repository. As you review your collection of publications, look for mold or insect damage. If there are any signs of damage, evaluate the materials and discard them as necessary. If a publication is important to your collection but has serious damage, contact a conservator for an assessment.

Before discarding duplicates or unwanted items, decide whether the duplicates would be useful to other institutions. Distribution lists such as the SAA's Archives and Archivist listserv is a good place to post information about unwanted materials. Often institutions may be willing to take the items off your hands for the cost of postage.

Processing Collections

For non-archivists or new archivists, you may wonder, what does it mean to "process" a collection? The act of processing a collection is akin to a librarian cataloging a book; however, processing involves much more than writing a simple catalog record for each item. Processing a collection means that you have organized the materials and created some sort of guide or catalog record to find the items within a collection. For those trained as archivists, processing may also mean preservation of a collection by removing the staples, putting papers in acid-free files in acid-free boxes, and creating a traditional finding aid. Although this sounds simple enough, it requires a lot of time and resources to process even a small collection in the traditional archival sense.

When it comes to processing collections, lone arrangers must learn to let go a little bit. So what does that mean? If you have had formal training in archives, you may need to give up the idea of fully fleshed out finding aids in favor of simpler inventories or box lists. Another tactic employed by many archivists is a new theory called "More Product, Less Process," or MPLP.[9] Unveiled in 2005 by Mark Greene and Dennis Meissner, this approach allows archivists to manage their backlogs by spending less time on the details and more time on the larger organizational needs. Small archives will always be faced with a backlog; therefore, lone arrangers have eagerly embraced this method as a way to process collections without getting hung up on the details. This method may not work for every collection, but you should consider it to help you reduce your backlog.

The MPLP method of processing eliminates item-level description in favor of keeping the materials within their original files in original order while describing only the larger group of records and providing a folder list. Because most collections come to us in original order in folders within boxes, we only need to create a box list and generate a broad description of the entire collection. This means focusing less on pulling staples, reboxing, and refoldering and more on description of the materials.

To achieve this level of processing, determine if the collection came to you in the order in which it was created. In some cases you will get files that are haphazardly thrown into a box and it is clear that this was not the original order. You can then arrange the folders alphabetically and/or chronologically, whichever is most appropriate. Once the folders are in order, place them in the box. If the folders came in a box that doesn't fit on your shelves or is badly damaged, replace the box. You may need to refolder some materials if they came to you in hanging file folders. Make a list of all of the folder titles in each box. If the files were labeled using stickers that fell off or are about to fall off, relabel those folders using pencil. Number the boxes and list the folders that correspond to that box. Finally, generate a basic description of the collection based on the information you have available.

{ KEY TERMS

A **finding aid** is a tool that assists in the discovery of information within a collection. It also provides a description of records that allows the repository to maintain physical and intellectual control over the materials. A finding aid can be found in multiple formats, including card indexes, calendars, guides, inventories, shelf and container lists, and registers. It is "a single document that places the materials in context by consolidating information about the collection, such as acquisition and processing; provenance, including administrative history or biographical note; scope of the collection, including size, subjects, media; organization and arrangement; and an inventory of the series and the folders.[10]

Processing a collection means that you have organized the materials and created some sort of guide or catalog record to find the items within a collection.

When deciding how to process a collection, keep in mind the following items:

- How will people access the collection? Will they access it through an existing catalog or database? Will they be looking for finding aids or collections through your website? Will the collections be described as part of a regional or national collaborative effort that requires a specific format?

- How much detail is needed in the description of a collection? Does it make more sense to describe items with one collection-level record in an online catalog or database, or should you describe the collections down to the folder level?

- Should all collections be processed at the same level?

- How frequently are these collections accessed or have the potential to be accessed?

- Do the collections need to be rehoused in archival boxes?

Part of the small processing area in the Washington County Free Library Western Maryland Room, Hagerstown, Maryland. These boxes are part of the General Russell P. Hartle World War II Collection. *Photograph courtesy of Carol Appenzellar.*

If you are required to or feel that the only way to go is traditional processing with full description and a complete finding aid, you need to take one of two approaches. First, try to partner with a college or university with an archival or public history program and use interns to arrange and catalog collections. If none of these exist near your institution, you can also use volunteers, if your institution allows them.[11] If neither of these options work for you, then set aside time in your schedule to do the processing yourself. As someone who might only have a few hours a week to spend on this, you will need to find a time and place where you can work uninterrupted for several hours at a time. You may find that after a while this approach is not practical. If so, you may want to revisit the MPLP method.

Before you begin any kind of processing, prioritize your collections. You may need to wait a few months to decide which collections get the most use, either internally or externally. It is more important to organize your heavily used collections even if they aren't as interesting to you. Another way to approach this is to process collections that could be very useful to your constituency but are currently invisible to them. Often archives hold collections that could be of high research value for their constituency but no one knows that they exist. These are often referred to as "hidden collections." If you identify collections that you feel are important to either your institution or your researcher base, you can use those collections to increase your visibility and assist with fundraising for your institution. Make these collections a high priority for processing.

Once you have identified the collections for processing, streamline processing by creating a finding aid template. Having a template allows you to have a uniform style for your finding aids whether they are paper-based or electronic. If you plan to encode your finding aids using encoded archival description (EAD), be sure that the template includes all of the fields that you need. There is no harm in looking at other archives' finding aids to formulate your template.

Now that you have your template, assess the collection(s) that you plan to process:

- Are they purely paper?

- Do they contain photographs?

- Are there audio/visual materials?

- Are there objects, artwork, or other non-paper items?

How you organize and process the materials will depend on their format. At this point you need to establish whether or not you need any special materials to house these collections. To make your work more efficient and economical, identify and order any supplies needed before you continue processing the collection.

Once you have prioritized your collections and processed the materials and you have a finding aid, you can determine what you plan to do with that information. If you are creating rudimentary box lists, you may want to keep that information for yourself rather than publish it on the Web. If you plan to make the collections accessible to the public or other constituents, decide how you plan to get the information out there. If you have been formally trained as an archivist, you may be eager to get your finding aids up on the Web using

EAD; however, you may not have the means to do so. If you simply want to get the information out there, it is okay to post PDF documents on your website and worry about EAD later. If you are part of a library, you may want to put a collection-level record in your library's online catalog so that patrons know that the collection exists and is available for research. (We will discuss EAD and its challenges as well as archival collections management software more in depth in the next chapter.)

Above: A collection of glass plate negatives as they were found by the archivist after she was hired. These negatives were in the original acidic sleeves, stacked horizontally on wooden shelves that were sagging under the weight. **Below:** The same glass plate negatives after processing. They are now housed on metal shelving, in acid-free sleeves, inside acid-free boxes, on their edge. *Photographs courtesy of Allaina Wallace, National Snow and Ice Data Center, Boulder, CO.*

THE ABRAHAM LINCOLN LIBRARY AND MUSEUM

BY MICHELLE GANZ

In 1896 General Oliver Otis Howard founded Lincoln Memorial University (LMU), a small liberal arts college in Harrogate, Tennessee. The school's charter mandated that the university maintain a museum collection of Lincolniana (materials relating to Abraham Lincoln) and Civil War memorabilia. From 1896 until 1977, the collection was housed in a variety of locations on the LMU campus before settling into its permanent home in the Abraham Lincoln Library and Museum. The collection is one of the largest collections of Lincolniana in the world; yet in its 113-year lifetime there has been sporadic custodianship of the collection within university departments. It is only in the last ten years that anyone with archival training has been in charge of the two-dimensional segment of the collections.

In 1937, R. Gerald McMurtry came to LMU as a history professor and Lincoln Scholar. For the next thirty years Dr. McMurtry took the collection from a haphazard assortment of materials to a nationally recognized collection. When Dr. McMurtry left, the collection suffered from a lack of strong leadership.

After years of sporadic archival management, the museum hired a trained and certified archivist to help organize and catalog the massive collection. Five years later, the archivist moved on, leaving behind an archive in transition. It was another five years before a new archivist was hired to continue the work of the previous archivist.

On arrival at the archive, I needed to get a sense of the state of the archives. The first step was to establish how much of the collection was already cataloged and understand the previous arranger's methods. The survey allowed me to decide which sections of the archives required immediate attention and what could wait. It also provided me with a basic understanding of the dynamics of the collection and allowed me to create a plan of action.

The survey revealed a number of previous practices that did not conform to SAA standards. In most cases, I determined that the best course of action would be to leave things as they were rather than change the procedure. To maximize productivity, I had to establish a protocol for how to work around what was already done.

The previous custodians of the collection began cataloging collections in a variety of ways: some items were cataloged correctly while others were cataloged in a completely undecipherable way. Much of the collection was cataloged using accession numbers in an eighty-dot (80.) format to indicate items found in the collection and donated prior to 1980. This created a bit of a quandary, as we now cannot identify which items were "found in collection" and which ones were received in 1980. A large portion of the collection was cataloged in this manner, making it too late to go back and renumber the items. The question then became how to work around what had already been done, for good or bad. I decided to retain the "found in collection" numbering system, but I created a key to explain the numbering discrepancies. By creating a key of previous work done, I expanded access to the collection.

Once I gained a basic understanding of the peculiarities of the collection, I broke the whole collection into manageable projects. Then the task of cataloging almost 200,000 items seemed far less daunting. It also allowed for the creation of multiple access points to the collection, such as breaking down the collection into "sub-collections"—for example, the pamphlet collection, the photograph collection, and so on—and allowing the museum to highlight the most interesting parts of the collection to scholars and the general public.

Over the course of the last few years, I have had a learning curve; not all work came to fruition in the way I initially planned. Flexibility and compromise are necessary to make an archive a dynamic part of the museum as a whole. I will often have to move directly from Plan A to Plan H at a moment's notice. One example was a trove of lithographs collected by the same individual discovered in an uncataloged map case. I made the decision to give the collection one overarching accession number and to give each lithograph its own sub-collection number. I then individually numbered, foldered, and relocated the lithographs to a new drawer. A few months later more lithographs from the same collection were discovered. A few months after that even more were discovered. After two years, more than 1,000 lithographs were found. By that time, it was too late to go back and fix the organizational structure. In hindsight it would have been more cost- and time-effective to folder and group the lithographs by size and topic rather than individually. Each lithograph would have received its own individual number, but the cost of supplies needed would have been reduced to a fraction of current projected costs. The manpower costs to go back and redo the previous work are too high to make it a viable option.

Museum archives present their own problems and rewards. Creating an orderly usable collection out of chaos 115 years in the making has been a challenging task—one that has taught me to think beyond the standard way of doing things. It has shown me that every problem has a solution if you look hard enough, and every success is worth the effort.

Working with Other Institutions

Working in a small institution can be a challenge, but one that can become an opportunity in some cases. Depending on your situation, working with another institution, large or small, may benefit your institution but may also benefit you personally. Before entering into any type of partnership with another institution, get approval from your supervisor and any governing bodies that might have a say in such a relationship.

So what kind of partnerships are out there, and how can they benefit you? Institutions often partner on the following projects:

- Collection development

- Databases or other information technology (IT) issues

- Disaster planning

- Fundraising and grant writing

Each institution in a partnership can bring strengths to the table and coordinate efforts rather than struggling on its own. This isn't always feasible, perhaps because there aren't any other organizations nearby or because an institution has decided that it doesn't want any partners.

If your institution does partner with another institution on a project, your workload might ease but it may also increase. Before you go looking to partner with another archives, consider both the benefits and the consequences:

- Will the partnership ease budget concerns or create extra costs?

- Will it create more or less work?

- What are the benefits?

- Do the benefits outweigh the cost or workload?

Collaboration on databases or other IT issues may go hand-in-hand with your collection development policies and potential fundraising opportunities. Before agreeing to partner in an IT venture, collection development, or fundraising activities, determine your collecting scope and goals. You do not want to compete with another institution but rather work with them in a way that benefits you both. For example, if your institution and another court the same donors, a partnership with that institution may be problematic.

If you can collaborate and complement your collections by working together on collection development policies or through a joint database or institutional repository, the partnership can be beneficial. Collaboration may be required or advisable in some cases. For example, if your archives is located in a town or county that also has a museum and/or historical society and you are all collecting materials related to the history of that area, it is beneficial to all of these institutions to collaborate on collection policies and perhaps a unified catalog of materials that are available to researchers. Why fight over donations and patrons when you could work together?

By collaborating with another institution to create databases or install a software system to provide online access to your collections, you can increase your visibility while sharing some of the costs. For example, two or more smaller institutions can collaborate to create and maintain a photographic database or collections system. Smaller colleges and universities can establish or work through an already established collaborative to create joint catalogs, databases, and institutional repositories, such as Fenway Libraries Online or the Five Colleges.

Another mutually beneficial partnership may be disaster planning. If you live near other small archives, historical societies, or museums, you may benefit from assistance from these institutions when dealing with a disaster. Many small archives partner with each other and keep a contact list in case of an emergency. It is helpful to have other archivists on the scene of a disaster as they know how to handle the materials without damaging them further.

Fundraising, including grant writing, provides a mutual benefit by raising money to accomplish a goal that benefits both institutions. In most cases, institutions collaborate on grant projects that seek to develop or acquire a unique collection, process collections, or develop methods for providing access to those collections. Institutions can work together to raise money for oral history projects, processing projects, or digital collaboratives. Determine what type of project you want to pursue and seek out a compatible partner with similar goals and interests who is willing to collaborate. To be successful, you will need to work closely with your development departments. (For more information on fundraising and grant writing, see Chapter 7.)

Conclusion

Organizing and maintaining an archives is difficult work, especially when you have to do it alone, but there are ways of successfully managing the workload:

- Assess your situation and determine what policies and structure need to be put in place.

- Focus only on projects and tasks that are essential functions of your position and the archives.

- Once you have determined what is essential, begin to organize your collections by

  o Tracking new acquisitions

  o Documenting existing collections

  o Arranging and describing collections in a way that is useful to both you and the end user

When processing collections, arrange and describe them to the best of your abilities and to an appropriate level. Some collections may require more work than others. Prioritize your collections according to usage and importance to the institution. For those of us who have been formally trained as archivists, it is easy to focus too much on how something "should" be done while we lose sight of what really "needs" to be done. Look at archival standards as a goal to aim for, but don't feel as though you have failed if those goals are not met. When it comes to managing collections, any structure is better than no structure.

Consider whether or not collaborating with other institutions is feasible. If it is, determine what types of collaboration may work best for your institution and how it may benefit you and the other institutions involved. Working with other archivists toward similar goals can keep you from feeling isolated and give you confidence in the work that you are doing.

NOTES

1   Elizabeth Yakel outlined these steps in *Starting an Archives* (Chicago: Society of American Archivists; Metuchen, NJ: Scarecrow Press, 1994), 20. Yakel refers to Thomas Wilsted and William Nolte's *Managing Archival and Manuscript Repositories* (Chicago: Society of American Archivists, 1991), 29.

2   Richard Pearce-Moses, *A Glossary of Archival and Records Terminology* (Chicago: Society of American Archivists, 2005), available at http://www.archivists.org/glossary/index.asp.

3   Pearce-Moses, *Glossary*.

4   For more information on specific software options, see Appendix B. For a discussion of archival computer applications, see Chapter 3.

5   Pearce-Moses, *Glossary*.

6   F. Gerald Ham, *Selecting and Appraising Archives and Manuscripts* (Chicago: Society of American Archivists, 1993), 51–54.

7   Ibid., 58.

8   Pearce-Moses, *Glossary*.

9   Mark A. Greene and Dennis Meissner, "More Product, Less Process: Revamping Traditional Archival Processing," *American Archivist* 68 (Fall/Winter 2005): 208–263.

10 Pearce-Moses, *Glossary*.

11 For more information on using interns and volunteers, see Chapter 4.

CHAPTER 3

"How Do I Survive in the Digital Age?"
Information Technology Issues for Lone Arrangers

Archivists in small shops are facing big challenges in the digital age. Although using computers in an archival setting is not new, the variety of uses and the frequency of use has grown exponentially in the last decade. One area in which archivists may not be trained but are often expected to handle is information technology (IT) as it relates to archives and records management. How much you are expected to know or do depends on how your institution is organized.

Small institutions are familiar with the challenges of minimal staff and tight budgets, but the digital age has placed an added stress to the increasingly complicated role of the lone arranger. As more records are generated electronically, lone arrangers face enormous challenges in acquiring and preserving those records. In addition to these problems, archives are under pressure to make their holdings accessible by creating online databases or finding aids. In some cases, we are expected to digitize and place whole collections online.

Some institutions have IT staff readily available while others have no staff or centralized means of handling technical issues. If your institution does have IT staff or an administrator assigned to handle all IT matters, be sure to include them in any discussions relating to software, hardware, or website changes that you would like to undertake. It is important to invite them to any software demonstrations and share any technical requirements before purchasing software. You do not want to purchase something only to find out that you do not have the technical capability to run the application. If you do not have administrative rights to your computer or your institution's operating systems, you should not attempt any activity without the permission of your administrators or IT staff.

The common types of IT issues faced by lone arrangers include:

- Choosing an archival collections management system
- Choosing a digital asset management system

- Creating an institutional repository
- Setting up electronic document management systems
- Digitizing collections

This chapter explores these issues to clarify concepts and provide the groundwork for making decisions on how to survive and thrive in the digital age.

Archival Collections Management Systems

Often when archivists are trying to get a handle on their collections, the first thing they turn to is software. It is important to note the distinction between various software functions and not to confuse a collections management system with a content management system. This section discusses software related to collections management, which is designed to manage information *about* collections, not the collections themselves. Information that can be managed using a collections management system includes:

- Collection documentation
- Finding aids or four-level collection cataloging (i.e., collection, series, box, folder, or item)
- Accession records
- Donor information
- Loan records
- Condition reports
- Restrictions
- Patron information

Some systems allow you to store images, audio, and video content within the item record—making the system more versatile than a regular finding aid. (Appendix B offers a list of commonly used archival collection management systems.)

If this is the kind of software that you need, you must then ask, "Which software program should I use?" It is true that there are plenty of off-the-shelf software solutions, either those specifically designed for archival collections or those that can be easily adapted. What works for one institution won't necessarily work for another.

The following factors will play a key role in your decision:

- What do you want your database to do?
- Your comfort level with technology and knowledge of databases
- Is it easily adaptable?

It is important to note the distinction between various software functions and not to confuse a collections management system with a content management system.

- Do you need to pay an additional fee to have the software company configure the system to meet your needs?

- Does your institution have an IT department or person on site? If so, can your IT staff assist with support, setup, and configuration of the software?

- Your budget

Let's take a look at each of these factors.

Before you get started, determine why you want a collections management system and what you want it to do. If you are doing something simple, such as a box list or a running accession register, a simple Microsoft Excel spreadsheet, Microsoft Access database, or Microsoft Word document may be all that you need. If you are looking for something more complex that can manage multiple tasks, such as finding aids, accessions, donors, donations, and researchers, then you may need something more substantial.

Next, determine your comfort level with technology, software, and knowledge of setting up or configuring databases. If you are not comfortable with customizing software to meet your needs and you do not have an IT department, then you may want to find something simple that you can buy off the shelf, comes with technical support, and is user friendly. If you are more comfortable with configuring software and databases, you may want to use any number of more complex off-the-shelf or open source options, many of which are inexpensive or even free, that you can adapt to your needs.

If you have an IT department, talk to them about what might be possible using your current resources. Depending on the system and how you plan to use it, you need to determine if it has a Web interface and find out if it is compatible with your website. You also need to make sure that the software will be compatible with any other software that you might purchase. Some software may require specifications that your institution's current setup does not meet. If the software requires servers and operating systems that aren't in place, that is an additional expense to consider. If you don't have an IT department or even an IT person, you will need to find out whether or not you will be able to set up the software and maintain it on your own.

Last but not least, what is your budget? It may be easy to find the "perfect" software to meet your needs, but if you don't have the money it might not be so perfect. Keep in mind that although the initial purchase might be a one-time expense, you often need to pay additional, recurring fees to maintain the system with upgrades and technical support. You also need to bear in mind the stability of the software; is it something new and untested, or is it something that has been around for a while and has been proven to last? If you need to continually change software systems because the company no longer supports it or goes out of business, then you need to consider the financial cost as well as time and resources required to replace the software. Talk to colleagues at similar institutions that are using the software before making any decisions.

{ KEY TERMS

Open source software is defined by the *Glossary of Archival and Records Terminology* as computer code that is developed and refined through public collaboration and distributed without charge but with the requirement that modifications must be distributed at no charge to promote further development.[1]

If you have no money for software in your budget, a "free" option might be the way to go, either using an existing system, having your IT department create a "home-grown" solution, or using an open source solution. If you go with an open source or "home-grown" solution, you need to think about your time investment, both to set it up and to maintain it. One other problem with "home-grown" solutions is that if the person that sets up the database leaves the institution, there is no one left to assist with troubleshooting and maintenance.

The best way to approach your decision is to explore options. Look up software solutions online and talk to colleagues about their experiences. Keep the following questions in mind when reviewing software:

- Does the software do what I want it to do?
- What is required to make it work for me?
- What other institutions are using it? Are they similar in size and nature to mine?
- How much does it cost?

Software review requires contacting vendors and colleagues. Don't be afraid to contact a vendor even if you don't plan on purchasing anything in the immediate future. Vendors are often happy to talk to you about their product (which, of course, they will try to sell to you). If you feel that the software is something that will work for you, schedule a time when the vendor can visit and demonstrate the product. If you know other local archivists who might benefit from the demonstration, invite them as well. Invite your IT staff so that they can ask questions about the software. Talk to colleagues in similar institutions to find out what type of software they are using and whether or not they have used that specific product. A current user is always the best gauge of whether or not the software may be right for you.

Don't be afraid to contact a vendor even if you don't plan on purchasing anything in the immediate future. Vendors are often happy to talk to you about their product (which, of course, they will try to sell to you).

Encoded Archival Description (EAD)

Many archival collection management systems allow you to create EAD finding aids. If you are scratching your head at this acronym, you probably aren't alone. EAD, or "Encoded Archival Description," became an accepted standard by the Society of American Archivists in 1998 as a way to provide additional information or metadata for online finding aids. Metadata allows search engines to find information or terminology that might not be in the plain text of the finding aid. In 2002, as EAD became more widely used, the Society of American Archivists released new EAD standards, which many archives use today.

Many trained archivists have asked themselves, "Should I use EAD or not?" It seems that several of your colleagues are putting up neatly designed, searchable finding aids on the Web while you spend most of your time just trying to process collections. You are told that EAD is the future of finding aids and that it should be your ultimate goal when providing access to your collections. While this may be true, and something to aspire to, it is not always an option for archivists working in small shops.

Although there are open source and free resources available that allow archivists to encode finding aids using EAD, not all institutions allow or support these options. Archivists' Toolkit and Archon are freeware or open source systems that can assist you in the creation of EAD finding aids. As of 2011, these two systems are in the process of being combined to become a new system called Archives Space. Many lone arrangers have used Archon successfully to get their finding aids online. Archon may work for some, but it is not an option for everyone because an IT department may not support it or allow it to be used in conjunction with particular Web content. If that is the case at your institution, you may need to work with your IT department to come up with an alternative solution.

If no alternative solution is available, you can post your finding aids as PDF files or in basic HTML. Many archives, particularly smaller archives, go with this option and still allow users access to your holdings. Current PDF documents allow you to search within the document, which allows your finding aid to be discovered by any search engine. If your archive is part of a library that has an online catalog, you should also include a collection-level MARC record in the system to give researchers more ways to find your collection. When creating MARC records, include a link to any PDF documents or other information related to the collection that will allow the researcher to find out more about the collection beyond the catalog record. You can always use EAD at a later time when it may be a more viable option. The most important thing in the immediate future is that your patrons have some way of accessing information about your collections online.

Digital Assets Management Systems (DAMS)

Digital assets management systems, or DAMS, manage collections of digital objects that are part of permanent archival collections. Those collections may have been digitized or were born digital. If you want to manage large numbers of digital photographs, audio, or video recordings, you might be in the market for a DAMS.

DAMS can complement archival collection management systems by serving as the "back end" system. Simply put, this system can manage large amounts of digital data and can serve as an access point for your collections management software. DAMS can also function independently without the need for a collections management system. If you do decide that you want or need both a collections management system and a DAMS, before purchasing anything, find out whether or not the two systems you are considering will work together and are not redundant.

CASE STUDY

GETTING FINDING AIDS ONLINE

BY TAMARA GAYDOS

When I came to the Phillips Library at the Peabody Essex Museum, I continued to process manuscript collections as it had been done for dozens of years. I arranged a collection, typed a finding aid, and filed a copy of it in the black binders in the reading room for researchers to use. There were typed lists of collections, a handwritten accessions log, and cards in the card catalog. Having recently graduated from Simmons College Graduate School of Library and Information Science, I had been exposed to all of the latest technology: EAD (Encoded Archival Description), electronic records, digitized collections, and more. I was surprised that such a prestigious library was still in the "Dark Ages."

There was no money in the budget to purchase systems for archival collections management or software to create EAD finding aids. There was an existing cataloging system called Voyager, and I used that to create a MARC record for each new collection and then pushed it out to OCLC, thereby making that collection searchable on the Internet. However, I was only one person working part-time and there was no time to go back to enter thousands of records for existing collections. (In all fairness, my predecessor had entered about 200 records for collections.)

What enabled me to bring us into the twenty-first century was this: interns. Through Simmons College's GSLIS internship program, I was able to take on several interns each semester to do the actual processing while I entered MARC records. At first I went back and entered all of the accession items so that they could be found. Then I started item-level cataloging of our logbook collection. Eventually we applied for a grant to a national organization, which required all of the collections to be accessible online at a minimal level, so I just started cataloging full time (four days a week). At that point I had an assistant who helped out for several months and a colleague who also started cataloging many hours per week. The project has been long but rewarding. Researchers are coming into the library, having searched online first and found material that they want to examine. In addition, we have uncovered many hidden treasures during this project.

To place our finding aids online, we have created PDF files from two finding aids and embedded a link to them in the MARC record. It was a quick and easy way to get them online. These files are not as dazzling as EAD finding aids would look, but they are searchable and do the job. However, I am currently using a trial download of a software program called Oxygen to convert my finding aids to EAD. This time my interns are teaching me, because they have recently been using this software. It is a slow process to enter each finding aid into Oxygen, but it will become faster with practice. We currently have enough server space to accommodate a small number of finding aids, but if we were to convert every finding aid, we would have to purchase more servers.

If you are trying to decide if a DAMS is what you need, ask yourself the following questions:

- What types/formats of digital items do I have?

- How much digital material do I have?

- How are they currently accessed?

- Are they easily accessed?

- Am I charged with digitizing large amounts of materials?

If you have a large number of digital items, are acquiring digital records, or have been charged with creating a large amount of digital material, you should explore your options for a DAMS. Due to the large volume and complexity of managing digital items, these systems are often much more expensive than a simple database solution. For recommendations about types of systems that might work for your situation and budget, talk to other archivists in similar institutions working on similar projects. Contact vendors and get feedback from users of any products you intend to purchase. (You can also find a list of several available digital asset management systems in Appendix B.)

Institutional Repositories (IRs)

If a content management system or a DAMS is not what you are looking for, you may be in the market for an institutional repository, or IR. An IR is an online system that allows for collecting, preserving, and disseminating the intellectual output of an institution, particularly a research institution, in digital form. It allows you to capture, structure, provide access to, and preserve those digital materials produced by an organization or community.[2] Academic institutions began using IRs as a way to enable scholarly communities to share information in various formats, such as electronic theses and dissertations, image collections, data sets, e-prints, and courseware.[3] Some examples include DSpace, which was created by the Massachusetts Institute of Technology, and Fedora, which was created by Cornell University. IRs can also be considered electronic libraries.

IRs are open source software applications and can be linked to the Open Archives Initiative, which is an attempt to build an interoperability framework for archives containing digital content and to enhance access to electronic publications. These systems are generally used in academic settings and in organizations that generate electronic publications on a regular basis, such as e-books and scholarly publications.

Whether or not an IR is right for you often depends on the type of institution you work for. Colleges and universities typically use IRs as a means of distributing scholarly works. It allows them to disseminate digital content to a worldwide audience; maximize the visibility of the institution; showcase their creative output; curate digital output; provide workspace for collaborative and large-scale projects; encourage interdisciplinary approaches to research; facilitate sharing of digital teaching materials; and support student endeavors such as theses, dissertations, and e-portfolios.[4]

Before looking at setting up an IR, ask yourself the following questions:

- Does your institution produce large quantities of electronic publications, such as journals, theses/dissertations, or e-books?

- Are you responsible for maintaining and disseminating this type of information for your institution?

- Are these materials that your institution wants to be available publicly? If not, you will need to create or find a solution that allows you to encode the material for select audiences.

If you answered *yes* to any or all of these questions, you may want to set up an IR. If not, consider a DAMS or an electronic document management system for managing digital content.

Electronic Document Management Systems (EDMS)

An electronic document management system (EDMS) or enterprise content management (ECM) tools, provides technologies, and methods to capture, manage, store, preserve, and deliver digital content across an entire institution. These tools allow the management of an organization's unstructured information, wherever that information exists. This system takes your digital content throughout its life cycle—from its creation to the ultimate disposition of that content.[5] In relation to collection management systems, digital asset management systems, and institutional repositories, an EDMS or ECM serves a records management function more than an archival function.

If you are responsible for records management—particularly electronic records management—in addition to your duties as an archivist, you might be in the market for an EDMS. Before you begin researching these software solutions, you will need to answer these questions:

- Do you have a records management policy in place?

- Under that policy, are you responsible for electronic records management across the entire institution?

- Do you have an IT department, and what is its role in electronic records management?

If you answered *no* or you don't know the answer to any of these questions, it would be best to get concrete answers and a solid records management policy in place before attempting to set up an EDMS. You will need the full support of your general counsel's office (or your institution, through outside legal services) and internal IT office (if you have one).

Metadata

Most important to acquiring and preserving a digital record is controlling your metadata. Metadata is "data about data" and provides descriptive terminology about a record, such as proper names, dates, places, type, technical information, and rights. Metadata is similar to a tag or a keyword assigned to a piece of information that you might see on a blog or an online photograph. Metadata allows researchers to search for specific keywords, such as names, places, objects, and time periods. When a researcher is looking for a photo of a man with a dog, it is the metadata that allows the researcher to find that photograph.

Metadata can be used to define things such as photographs, audio/video files, documents, and any other digital file. This information is usually embedded or connected to the file so that if the file is transferred or copied, the information follows the digital object. The information contained in the metadata allows a user to identify the who, what, where, and when of the file he or she is viewing. It may be helpful to think of it as a permanent label for each digital object.

Archivists use several types of metadata formats. The most commonly used formats are Dublin Core,[7] MARC,[8] MODS,[9] TEI,[10] EAD,[11] and METS.[12] Each of these formats allows for different types of metadata to be entered into a document. The type of information may be

- Descriptive: title, author, summary, topic

- Technical and structural: file size, software needed, file types, or instructions

- Administrative: record number, record date, record source

- Rights: copyright ownership, use privileges

- Management: price paid, circulation, restrictions[13]

Many lone arrangers use Dublin Core as their preferred metadata standard because it is simple to use, it is widely accepted, and it can be used with other types of metadata standards. The type of metadata standard that you chose will depend on your long-term objectives, needs, and capabilities.

So why is metadata so important? Without it, digital items would become useless over time. For example, if you have a nineteenth-century photograph without a label, you might be able to identify a person, place, or thing by doing some research, but if that person, place, or thing is not identifiable, then that photograph is nothing more than a pretty picture. With digital photographs you often end up with hundreds of photographs with no metadata. You may get a series of photographs of a building taken recently by your public affairs office staff, who now wants to send the photos to the archives. Most likely the photos will come to you with little or no information. Maybe they will have information from the camera such as camera type, pixel size, and, if you are lucky, a date. What you won't get is the subject. If you were to load that into your system without adding any metadata and that building is demolished in the next ten years, someone in the year 2098 might find that picture and not recognize the building. He or she wouldn't know where it was located on campus or even if it was located on campus. Without metadata to provide context, the photo will have lost its documentary value over time.

Digitizing Collections

The explosion of digital media and easy access to online materials in the last decade has prompted constituents and governing bodies of many cultural institutions to take action by requesting that their collections go online. Lone arrangers are not immune to these requests. Sometimes archivists are asked to digitize on an as-needed basis and other times they are asked to digitize all or part of an entire collection. There are many ways to approach digitization, and each project will require different processes, standards, and outcomes. How your institution decides to approach digitization will depend on its missions and goals.

KEY TERMS }

Digitization is the creation of a digital surrogate from an original physical object. This does *not* include items that were born digital, such as a Word document or database.

There are many reasons for digitizing collections. Some of the more common reasons are to facilitate access, to create online exhibits, to fulfill researcher requests, or to support an internal business process. Once you have identified the reason for digitizing your collections, determine the feasibility of digitizing, providing access, and preserving the digital files. You must also seriously consider any copyright or intellectual property rights issues that may prevent you from digitizing materials. If you are not sure of an item's copyright status, consult *Copyright & Cultural Institutions: Guidelines for Digitization for U.S. Libraries, Archives, & Museums* by Peter B. Hirtle, Emily Hudson, and Andrew T. Kenyon.[15]

There are several other factors that will influence how items will be digitized. Photographic prints must be scanned differently from photographic negatives or slides. Documents come in many sizes, and different types of documents and sizes may require different devices for digitizing. The fragility of items may also affect how you digitize them. If you plan to digitize bound items, you need to decide if they should remain bound or be unbound. Scanning audiovisual materials is more complicated. These collections require proper identification of format, stability of the material (Are the materials showing signs of deterioration?), and proper equipment to convert the materials into digital files.

After reviewing the materials to be digitized and establishing how you will manage the content, conduct your own cost-benefit analysis to determine if the project should be done in-house or outsourced to a company with experience digitizing the types of materials you want to include in your project. Consider the following costs:

- Your time: Figure out how much you are paid on an hourly basis and multiply that by the number of hours you think you will need to manage, prepare, and/or digitize collections.

- IT staff time: If you are using internal IT staff to assist you with the project, estimate the cost of their time as well.

- Software/hardware costs: Price any software or hardware you may need to complete the project.

- Other equipment or materials: Price any other items that you may need to complete the project, such as scanners, cameras, camera stands, tape decks, and so on.

- Cost of preparing materials: You may need to send fragile materials to a conservator or preservation specialist before digitization.

- Outside estimates: If you are going to outsource the project, get an estimate from the company as to how much it will cost for the digitization, shipping and handling (if applicable), and supplies.

Now that you know what you plan to digitize and have considered how you will digitize those materials, you need to decide how you will store, manage, and provide access to those files. If you have IT staff, involve them in the selection and setup of any software or hardware that may be purchased to complete the project. If you need to purchase software or create an in-house content management system, determine what you need that system to do. Ask yourself the following questions:

- Why are you digitizing these materials?

  o   For an online exhibit

  o   For individual research requests

  o   For an online searchable database of digital objects

  o   To facilitate internal business transactions

- Is the system for internal use only, or do you plan to export items to your website?

- Do you need the system to watermark items or only provide a thumbnail image to control usage of that image?

- How do you want to display the items, and how do you want patrons to access them?

Answers to these questions will allow you to begin exploring software and hardware options. You may not find a system that will meet all of your needs, so prioritize your system requirements. The software that you choose may also influence the hardware that you will need. Confirm that software and hardware are compatible before making any purchases.

Although each institution may approach digitization differently, there are some general guidelines that will apply to most situations. Do not digitize just because "everyone else" is doing it. Do it only if there is a clearly defined need to digitize items within your collection. It is important to stress the cost of resources, such as people, technology, and time, needed to accomplish even a small digitization project.

Break all potential projects into clearly defined steps. These steps include:

- Project planning and management: who is responsible for which steps of the project

- Pre-digitization preparation: acquire and set up any software/hardware, select items, prepare them for digitization

- Digitization: creating a digital surrogate, adding metadata, uploading the image to your DAMS or other content management system.

- Post-digitization: quality control of images and metadata, transferring data to other systems such as websites, or backup systems, long-term preservation of digital objects

Thoroughly document each of these steps so that if you cannot devote undivided attention to the project or you leave the job during the project, it can be continued by others. Include any technical requirements in your documentation.

If you are planning to digitize collections in-house, you need to have clearly defined technical requirements. These are guidelines that will define things such as file type (e.g., TIFF, WAV, PDF/A, etc.), resolution, color management or correction, and file naming.[16] Set up your workflow by incorporating the following steps:

- Before scanning anything, set up your digital repositories. You should have two storage areas, one on a local hard drive and one on a server.

  o Include enough storage space on your drives and/or servers to accommodate the file sizes generated by the project.

  o Keep one set of digital files as the preservation copy and the other for use.

  o Determine what, if any, software you need to fulfill the terms of the project.

- Set up your overall plan by prioritizing the materials that you plan to digitize.

- Test scan your materials to work out the best settings and determine how long it will take to scan each item.

- Set a schedule for yourself. This may mean setting aside several hours once or even a few times a week to dedicate to the project.

Do not digitize just because "everyone else" is doing it. Do it only if there is a clearly defined need to digitize items within your collection.

- Create two sets of files, one larger preservation file (in TIFF format) and a use copy, generally a JPEG file.

- Embed any metadata into the files so that they are searchable.

Once you have your equipment and workflow established, you can begin scanning. Resolve all hardware and software issues before beginning a project. When digitizing materials, include metadata with the digital objects so that they will be searchable over time. In addition to metadata, you need to have a preservation plan in place to ensure that your digital objects are safe and will be accessible in the future. Preservation should also be a key component in any digitization project.

Conclusion

Technology can be both a great help and a great hindrance for a lone arranger. It can save you time but can also create problems if projects are not well planned and executed. If you have an IT department, work with them closely to identify your needs and take advantage of the help they may be able to provide. If you do not have an IT department, be sure to utilize systems that you can set up and manage on your own. To facilitate organization and access of materials, you may need to look into more than one information technology solution to achieve your goal.

Acquiring, creating, and managing digital content is a serious commitment of both time and resources. Use those resources wisely by setting reasonable goals and putting in place the proper guidelines and technologies that will allow you to efficiently and effectively complete a project before you start. If you do decide to set up a system to manage your digital content, think about how you will manage it and maintain it. Don't forget to incorporate metadata within your digital objects. Metadata is an important factor in preservation, storage, and retrieval of digital files. If it is not included with your files, they will lose value over time.

NOTES

1 Richard Pearce-Moses, *A Glossary of Archival and Records Terminology* (Chicago: Society of American Archivists, 2005), available at http://www.archivists.org/glossary/index.asp.

2 Ibid.

3 Ibid.

4 Alma Swan, *Open Access Institutional Repositories: A Briefing Paper,* http://www.openscholarship. org/upload/docs/application/pdf/2009-01/open_access_institutional_repositories.pdf.

5 Bryant Duhon, "Enterprise Content Management: What Is It? Why Should You Care?" *AIIM E-Doc Magazine* 17, no. 6 (November/December 2003).

6 Pearce-Moses, *Glossary.*

7 For more information about Dublin Core, see http://dublincore.org/metadata-basics/.

8 For more information on MARC, see http://www.loc.gov/marc/.

9 For more information on MODS, see http://www.loc.gov/standards/mods/.

10 For more information on TEI, see http://www.tei-c.org/index.xml.

11 For more information on EAD, see http://www.loc.gov/ead/.

12 For more information on METS, see http://www.loc.gov/standards/mets/.

13 Eric Childress, "Metadata Standards," presented at the FEDLINK OCLC Users Group Meeting, Washington, DC, November 18, 2003, http://www.oclc.org/research/presentations/childress/ fedlink_20031118.ppt.

14 Ibid.

15 A PDF version of this document is available online at http://ecommons.cornell.edu/.

16 Sample technical guidelines can be found at http://www.digitizationguidelines.gov/guidelines/ digitize-technical.html or http://memory.loc.gov/ammem/about/techIn.html.

CHAPTER 4

"How Am I Going to Get My Work Done?"
Fundamental Archival Programs

Archival programs require planning whether you are a one-person shop or have an extensive staff. Planning your programs will help you control the growth and longevity of your collections. Programs that are essential to your archives' success are

- Preservation planning

- Internship or volunteer programs

- Records management

Creating these plans can be a challenge; enforcing them within your institution can be even more so. It is important to make the case to your supervisors that these are essential functions to a successful archival program.

Without the support of your institution and your constituency, it will be difficult to get these programs in place. To gain support, you need to make a strong case for each of these programs, addressing the following:

- Why the program is important

- How it supports the mission of your archives

- Who it will benefit

- What will happen without it

How you present your case will depend on your situation; however, you should show examples of both successful and unsuccessful programs. To find examples, contact your colleagues at conferences and meetings, through listservs, networking sites, by phone, by mail, or by e-mail.

Preservation Planning

Preservation planning can mean any number of things, depending on the institution. It might mean starting from scratch, trying to acquire or modify storage spaces to meet minimum preservation standards; or it may mean setting up disaster plans and conserving the most important collections. The more resources available, the more elaborate the plan can be. Traditionally, workers in small shops lack the staff and internal resources to deal with materials that need extensive preservation or conservation, but that doesn't mean that we should leave out preservation planning. Simple steps can greatly extend the life of collections.

It is best to have a comprehensive preservation plan in place. In a small shop it is often difficult to find the time to write such a plan. In most cases, it is more important to do something than to write something. You could spend a lot of time writing an elaborate preservation plan, but if it will never be used or implemented, that plan is worthless. Do a quick survey of your space and then your collections. There are several steps in this process:

- Determining your physical space

- Establishing a preservation policy

- Creating a budget for preservation

- Evaluating your progress

Determining Your Physical Space

Start by conducting a brief survey of your physical space and identifying characteristics associated with the environment. What kind of storage conditions do you have physically and environmentally?

Monitor the temperature and humidity of your collections throughout the year. A hygrothermograph (a machine that reads temperature and humidity) will help you accomplish this goal. Some archival suppliers have inexpensive digital readers that will display temperature and relative humidity. They may not be as accurate as more expensive pieces of equipment, but it will tell you the basic environmental conditions. You can track the changes over time by creating a spreadsheet and taking readings on a regular basis (once a week/ every two weeks). Then you will know whether the environment in your storage area changes with the seasons.

If your storage space has excessive heat (multiple days over 75 degrees Fahrenheit) or high humidity (higher than 50 or 60 percent), there are simple steps you can take to remedy the situation. Purchase a dehumidifier to lower the humidity in your space. To cool the space, do not open windows (if you have them); instead, turn down the temperature on your HVAC system or request that it be lowered. This might be a challenge if your area is cooled on the same system as other offices. If it is, ask if you can buy a small room air conditioner to keep the archives storage space cooler.

Light is an important factor in determining the life span of collections. Lighting not only fades collections; it can also produce heat, which will make your HVAC system work harder. If your collections are exposed to direct or indirect sunlight from windows in your storage space, block those windows with blackout shades or other materials. Even if you don't have any windows, you need to assess your lighting:

- Are the lights on all of the time? Turn off lights in the archives when no one is using the room, or purchase motion sensor lights that automatically turn off after a certain amount of inactivity. This will also reduce electricity costs.

- What kind of lights do you have? If you have fluorescent lighting, purchase filters to block ultraviolet rays from damaging your materials. In some cases it is a matter of switching the type of light bulb used in the archives to something that produces fewer ultraviolet rays.

Look around the space. Are there exposed pipes, leaks, mold, insects, vermin, or other undesirable conditions? If you see evidence of any of these problems, address them *immediately*! Hiring pest control or putting your space on your institution's list for pest management can easily address some of these issues. Ask your maintenance team to fix leaks or other mechanical problems or structural issues. Increased or regular maintenance of the area will improve overall conditions.

If your storage area is located in a basement that has flooded in the past, seek an alternate location, if possible. Shelving that can be adjusted to keep records above any potential floodwaters can protect a collection that must be stored in the basement. When new shelving is not an option, use palettes or similar platforms to get boxes off the floor. Even a few inches of height could save your collections from a flood. You can also buy water detection systems and boxes with a special coating to help reduce the risk of water damage.

Once you have assessed the storage area, take a look at how you store your materials. Are your materials shelved, and how? If your records are in a pile on the floor, you may need to start at square one. Appropriate shelving should hold not only document cases but also record storage boxes and other larger materials. Traditional library shelving is not deep enough to accommodate archival boxes. If possible, locate or purchase metal shelving with a baked enamel finish. Make sure that the shelving holds the weight of several full archival boxes. Each shelf should be able to hold 150 to 200 pounds. If you cannot afford "archival" shelves, work with what you can afford from your local office supply store.

It is also important to consider your floor load. If your space is not designed to hold shelves with up to 1,000 pounds per section (meaning your floor must hold multiple thousands of pounds of weight), then you need to search for a new space. Before purchasing shelving, speak with your supervisor about your concerns regarding the load-bearing capacity of your space.

One final consideration is cleanliness. It is important to keep the storage space clean from dust, debris, and other potentially damaging materials. Purchase a vacuum with a HEPA (high-efficiency particulate air) filter and "dust" regularly.

The current archivist found this archives in complete disarray. *Photograph courtesy of Robert Antonelli, University of Portland.*

You can also help minimize dust and dirt by requesting that HVAC filters be changed regularly. Ask that a member of the maintenance staff come through the storage area with your guidance to clean the floors and stack areas, making sure that they do not use harsh chemicals or splash water on the collections. If the maintenance staff is unable to assist you, buy a broom and dust pan and periodically make a quick pass through the aisles to clean up any debris lying in the stacks.

Your physical space is important, not only for the collections but also for the safety of you and others working in and around the archives. It might be difficult to make your case for better storage conditions, but it is important to remember that you were hired for your professional abilities, and that includes your professional opinions and observations.

Establishing Preservation Priorities

Once you have determined your space and the kind of shelving you are going to use, take a look at your collections. Are they thrown in boxes or simply piled on shelves or the floor? Make decisions by gathering information about your collections and the potential problems and solutions needed to remedy any less-than-ideal situations. If your collections are in disarray, spend time boxing small sections so that they won't get damaged until you have time to process and properly house them. Keep in mind that your budget will determine how you will ultimately house your materials. Prioritize collections or items; those that are important to the institution or are in dire condition should be put on the top of the list for conservation work, proper housing, or both.

When prioritizing collections, identify which items need conservation work and which media in your collections require transfer to another medium to be accessible for years to come. You may select large sections of your collections for further preservation/conservation that will have to be outsourced. Consider setting aside a portion of your budget each year to do one or more preservation projects or seek small grants for specific conservation projects. If you have a large group of records from a single collection, you can preserve it by working through a set number of items each year until the project is done.

Preservation can mean something as simple as putting often-used photographs in Mylar or Melinex sleeves or putting a book with a broken spine into a phase box (a special box designed to hold and support books). The physical conservation of materials is much more involved and requires special training. If any items in your collection are damaged by water, mold, or insects or are brittle, they may need the attention of a trained conservator. Often conservators are trained in a particular specialty, such as paper, photographs, media, binding, or art. If you need the services of a conservator, check with other archivists or consult the American Institute for Conservation[1] or the resource guide located in Appendix B of this book. Most of your collections will only need preventive care or preservation, while only a small portion of your collections might require conservation.

Identify potentially hazardous materials within the archives. If your collection contains weapons or other potentially dangerous items, contact your local fire department or police department for assistance. Although these items may be old, they may still be capable of detonation or explosion. Only an expert can determine if the item is safe.

Other potential hazards are nitrate films and negatives. Nitrate was used roughly between the 1890s and 1950s. It deteriorates rapidly and can be very unstable and combustible if stored in warm and humid climates. According to Monique Fischer's "A Short Guide to Film Base Photographic Materials: Identification, Care, and Duplication," you may have nitrate film if it is exhibiting any of these characteristics:

- The negatives are beginning to yellow and mirror.
- The film becomes sticky and emits a strong noxious odor. (Note: If you smell a strong vinegar smell, it is most likely cellulose acetate film and not nitrate film.)
- The film can become an amber color and the image begins to fade.
- The film is soft and can weld to adjacent negatives, enclosures, and photographs.
- The film can degenerate into a brownish acid powder.[2]

If you have determined that you have nitrate films in your collection, separate them from the other collections immediately and contact a conservator.

Creating a Preservation Budget

Budgeting in a small shop can be tricky. Sometimes you aren't given a budget and are simply told that you will be granted money on an "as needed" basis determined by a manager or board. In other cases, you may be given a blanket

Martha Wachsmuth shows off the new compact shelving with most of the materials now properly housed and organized into archival boxes. *Photograph courtesy of Robert Antonelli, University of Portland.*

{ KEY TERMS

Conservation is the repair or stabilization of materials through chemical or physical treatment to ensure that they survive in their original form as long as possible.[3]

Preservation is the professional discipline of protecting materials by minimizing chemical and physical deterioration and damage to minimize the loss of information and to extend the life of cultural property or the act of keeping from harm, injury, decay, or destruction, especially through noninvasive treatment.[4]

budget for the year that you will need to manage carefully. If you are lucky, you might be able to negotiate your budget allocations. As part of the management of the budget, set aside money for preservation activities.

It may take a year or more before you can decide how much you can and should allocate to your preservation budget. First, make a list of high-priority items and rank them; then determine the costs associated with those items. You may find that you need to adjust your priority list based on those costs. This is a back-and-forth process as you continually adjust to meet your needs and your budget. If you have no preservation budget, consider partnering with other departments in your institution that may have extra dollars to spend toward preserving archival materials that suit their interests or needs. (For more information on budgeting, see Chapter 7.)

Service volunteer Kelsey Farrand and Sr. Sally Witt take digital photos of pages of a pre-1900 book of receipts and expenses for the Sisters of St. Joseph. *Photograph courtesy of the Sisters of St. Joseph, Alyson Walls Photographer.*

Evaluating Your Progress

The final step is to evaluate your progress. This is a multi-step process that will happen over time. Working in a small shop, you have to take tiny steps; as you work your way through the plan, it may not look like you accomplished what you set out to do, but you may have accomplished more than you think. Each year, reflect on what you have accomplished. Have you met your preservation goals? Why or why not?

If you determine that you have met your goals, that means that they were attainable when you set them. If you have not met your goals, consider what you initially set out to do. Did you partially attain your goals? If you didn't fully meet the goals, was it because of something you did or did not do or was there an outside factor that you could not control? Don't beat yourself up for not being able to get that painting restored or 500 linear feet of materials reboxed. Refocus, reassess, and create new goals. Just like your budget, you need to adjust to changes in your workload, priorities, and budget.

Internship and Volunteer Programs

Internship and volunteer programs are an important part of a lone arranger's repository. You can certainly run the archives without volunteers and interns, but extra hands lighten the load. If you work for a college or university, you may also get student workers to assist you. There are advantages and disadvantages to having an internship and/or volunteer program.

Providing internships to students may not be an option for you due to location or other factors. Some institutions do not allow interns to work for them because of liability or other issues. More importantly, you may not have students available. If you are located far from any colleges or higher-education institutions, an internship program may not be feasible. On occasion, you may have a student request an internship between semesters that may or may not be for credit.

If you are able to recruit interns or volunteers, you can gain extra help with little or no financial cost. You can train interns or volunteers to work on a specific project or to assist with multiple projects or tasks. The amount of training and tasks assigned should be proportionate to the length of time that you expect your interns or volunteers to work for you. A volunteer may stay longer, and you can often schedule his or her time and establish a routine.

Interns often require more than just time from you, however; internships should be structured and provide an opportunity for students to be mentored by a professional archivist. In addition, internships should be supervised and evaluated both by you and someone from the student's institution. Remember that you are providing a valuable resource both to the student and the school that the student is attending.

Paperwork is part of the price you pay when taking on an intern. Plan to write at least one report on the intern's progress or success. Also, you should write a document—not too lengthy or detailed—that explains the guidelines you have set for the internship. Assign projects that will permit the student to work independently but will challenge him or her and offer valuable experience. Basic processing projects work best. You will, however, need to assess the student's progress and check in with him or her for questions. Some interns and volunteers are better at asking questions than others. Be sure that students understand your instructions and are following the protocol that you have established. If you do take interns, expect to serve as a reference for other internships or their first jobs out of school.

Usually interns are required to work on one specific project within a limited number of hours. Be sure that the project that you assign is realistic given these constraints. Keep in mind that some students and volunteers work more efficiently and may complete their projects before they complete their hours and others may not finish their projects at all. Be prepared to pick up where they left off as needed or plan small, related projects for those who finish early. When choosing projects for volunteers and students, gauge their interests and test their abilities. If a student or volunteer is engaged in work in which he or she is truly interested, that person will perform better and will be more efficient.

When interns are not an option, volunteers may be a way to get assistance. Volunteers can be a mixed blessing. Some may be quick learners, efficient, and adapt well to archival responsibilities, while others may not be as well suited to archival work. Interview volunteers to determine what skills they have and try to match those skills with a project. Have them start with smaller test projects to establish how their skills mesh with archival work. Choose projects that will

PRESERVATION PLANNING FOR LONE ARRANGERS

BY JEREMY LINDEN

SUNY Fredonia, a predominately undergraduate institution within the State University of New York, was founded as the Fredonia Academy in 1826, and since that time it has served not only as a focal point for education and the training of teachers within the region but has also built an Archives and Special Collections program that goes far beyond the scope of campus and local history. Archives and Special Collections can trace its roots back to the arrival of the Stefan Zweig Collection in 1969 and the creation of the Local History Collection in 1971. It now houses the University Archives, local history collections, and major collections regarding Zweig, the Holland Land Company, saxophonist Sigurd Rascher, and the Coalition for West Valley Nuclear Wastes.

Managed part-time by librarians early on, in 1986 the university hired a part-time curator to lead the department, while other librarians served as project directors for other collections. In 2006 the university hired its first head of Archives and Special Collections. The department is currently staffed by the head of Archives and Special Collections, one library clerk, a part-time coordinator for the Zweig Collection, and a librarian who works half-time with the department.

Like many small repositories, preservation at SUNY Fredonia has historically occurred at the collection or item level, with little high-level strategic planning. Preservation was a recognized mandate and was listed as the primary role of the department in the original, and subsequent, collection policies. Nonetheless, the absence of any cohesive approach to preservation at a departmental level resulted in a variety of practices among the different collections, media types, and storage areas. Actual preservation results ranged from collections that were well prepared but stored in substandard environmental conditions to collections whose contents demanded far more attention than they were given.

We began our initial preservation planning process in 2006. Previous staff established basic physical control of the collections in five storage areas. Intellectual control varied from collection to collection and media type to media type. First we examined the existing departmental policies and procedures to confirm that preservation was included in the role of Archives and Special Collections and that the information was being clearly communicated to the administration of the university for mandate and budgetary purposes. Then we conducted a basic preservation needs survey of the collections. Given our small staff size compared to the extent of the collections, a full preservation survey was unrealistic. Instead, we chose to concentrate on a series of high-level, collection type, and media type surveys. The departmental role, and the benefit of preservation, was clarified where necessary, with documentation created where it was lacking. This first step, while seemingly simple, is what allows for continued planning and expenditure, in terms of resources, for the preservation mission.

The second of these surveys was an inspection of the environment within our repository storage areas, recognizing that our ability to control it has a far greater impact on our ability to preserve materials over time than preservation rehousing. At the university, we manage seven primary storage areas spread through three separate but attached buildings served by four different air-handling systems. Our environmental conditions vary from one storage area to another, and the level of environmental control that can be established ranges from direct control (the air handler that only services our department) to no control (the air handlers that service units or areas other than our department). To this end, we secured funding through the National Endowment for the Humanities Preservation Assistance Grant to purchase Preservation Environment Monitors and the Climate Notebook software from the Image Permanence Institute. The data from these monitors will be used to make strategic planning decisions regarding the storage of various collections and media types according to temperature and relative humidity conditions in the different storage areas. It will also be used to advocate for changes to our storage areas over time. As collection and media-specific preservation procedures are completed, we will achieve a systematic approach to long-term environmental storage options for those materials.

The next step was to concentrate on collection and media types. As before, the limitation was that we could not realistically survey the entirety of the collections while continuing the daily workflow performed by a small staff. Our two guiding principles at each stage of preservation planning are context and priority: what we can realistically achieve, what is appropriate in the context of our small repository, and what our priorities should be.

A key example of this intersection was our digitization of the Holland Land Company Maps in 2007 and 2008. We were faced with a simultaneous preservation and access problem. SUNY Fredonia holds the single, master copy of color microform maps (on microfiche and microfilm) created from original maps held in Amsterdam, the Netherlands. These maps, an invaluable resource to researchers in the United States and abroad, presented two problems. The color maps on microfiche were essentially inaccessible due to the format; the maps took up the entirety of the card, and only a fraction was visible at any one time through a fiche reader. Preservation concerns were based on the nature of the color film and the fact that the master copy was also the use copy. In this case, the decision was that digitization would benefit both preservation and access and that these items, due to their content and fragility, were a priority. Based on that decision, we successfully sought out grant funding to cover the costs of digitization. The master microforms are now safely in storage, with a master digital image stored on a secure server and an accessible image and metadata available through a Web interface.

Our procedures and practices have changed due to our preservation planning. Students working on processing collections are now trained in basic preservation practices to prevent the need for additional preservation measures in the future. Collections that were hastily processed in the past are being reprocessed to ensure proper preservation. We are inspecting how our departmental policies and procedures impact preservation, what the needs of our collection are, and how those needs can best be met given our resources and abilities. This allows SUNY Fredonia to consistently plan for the appropriate preservation of our collections on into the future.

not cause harm to your collections, such as creating forms, basic filing, moving boxes, creating box lists or inventories, and so on. If your volunteers have other skills, such as website or database design, you may want to have them work in that capacity.

It is important to keep in mind that you are not committed to keeping interns or volunteers. They are not paid and often have no recourse if you decide to let them go. The worst thing you could do for yourself is to keep an intern or volunteer that is causing you a great deal more work or causing harm to your collections. You may, however, find that you must keep an intern or a volunteer, either because the school requires that the intern finish or because politics within your institution prevents you from dismissing the volunteer. Then it is best to find a project that will keep him or her busy without causing you extra work. Balancing your work with the demands of interns and volunteers is not easy, which is why you should look at the pros and cons before starting such a program.

Ashley Judson, intern at the Emerson College Archives, works on creating boxes for fragile books. *Photograph courtesy of Emerson College.*

Planning Internships and Volunteer Programs

Before you jump into an internship or volunteer program, you need to do some basic planning. Create a list of needs according to priority. An excellent resource that addresses internship programs is Jeannette Bastian and Donna Webber's *Archival Internships*. (See Appendix A for publication information.)

As indicated previously, first ask yourself, "Do I have support from my department or institution?"[5] Some institutions will not support the use of interns because of liability or the perception that they will cause more work than benefits. The next step is to ask yourself, "Do I have appropriate projects?"[6] Continue with the following questions:

- Do you want a particular collection processed?

- Do you want items scanned?

- Do you need to conduct an inventory?

- Do you want to develop a brochure for the archives or event?

- Do you need someone to conduct provenance research?

- Do you need files labeled or moved?

- Do you want to record oral histories?

- Do you need to create an anniversary booklet?

- Do you have one large project or a series of smaller projects?

Keep a list of your answers on hand and then dissect your project into smaller components.[7]

Once you have completed your assessment, begin planning an internship or volunteer program that will work for you. If you decide that you are lacking the resources, skills, or appropriate workload, think about how you might be able to remedy the situation. Don't rush into a program if you are not ready, willing, or able to provide the best experience for both you and the intern or volunteer.

Now that you have decided to develop an internship or volunteer program, you need to prepare yourself and your institution for implementation. Start by laying down ground rules for the program. These rules should include topics such as cell phone and e-mail use while working, which areas are permissible to access, lunch hours, breaks, parking, attire, behavior, any terms for dismissal, and emergency preparedness instructions.

Once you have established rules, set up worksheets and forms that you will need to evaluate the success of the program. You will need a contact sheet for each person that volunteers or does an internship, and this can be attached to a resume, if you require one. Other factors to consider are time sheets, training materials, and any evaluation forms that you create or that are sent over by the student's school. Prepare an announcement, applications, and interview questions. If you plan to recruit students/volunteers at an internship/volunteer fair, create brochures or posters announcing the details of your internship or volunteer opportunities.

Now that you have done the preparation, you need to determine the following:

- Who will you send the announcement to?

- When will you send the announcement?

- What kind of experience can the student or volunteer expect?

- Where will the interns/volunteers work?

Start recruiting students or volunteers at least three months before your project begins; four to six months is ideal. If you are recruiting interns, be aware of academic schedules. If you are working with graduate students in an MLS program, the school may determine how interns are recruited.

Send a copy of internship announcements to the career development office and the degree program offices (which you determined earlier) for colleges in your region. If you recruit high school students, you need to contact the school guidance counselor. If you've built a rapport with specific individuals, route copies to them. Listservs are excellent means of distributing internship announcements, as are professional conferences.

VOLUNTEERS IN THE SMALL NONPROFIT INSTITUTION
BY PEG POESCHL SICILIANO

The History Center of Traverse City, formerly known as the Traverse Area Historical Society, is located in the northwest part of lower Michigan. It maintains more than 500 linear feet of archival materials and hosts a website on which much of its collection can be searched. It also provides ten public programs a year, publishes books and a quarterly newsletter, and designs four small exhibits for display at the local Museum of History.

Paid staff includes a fifteen-hour-a-week archivist and an eight-hour-a-week newsletter and layout specialist. This staff's ability to fulfill the above list of activities is due only to the hard work of twenty dedicated volunteers. An examination of the History Center's recruitment and retainment of this growing volunteer force will provide helpful guidance to other small organizations.

Volunteer Recruitment

New History Center volunteers appear from three sources: people who have seen History Center images in the local media or at local businesses, people invited by current volunteers, and people going through internship programs. The History Center also runs requests for volunteers in our newsletter and on our website, but in four years only one response has come through either source.

There is one essential key to attracting "drop by" volunteers through images in the media or at businesses. An organization must make sure it receives proper credit each and every time its materials are used. Patrons using multiple images are encouraged to put acknowledgements next to each image used, rather than using a one-time credit at the beginning or end of a publication. This significantly increases the number of times viewers see the History Center's name.

Also, staff and volunteers make a point to look through publications and drop by businesses that use our images. This creates an opportunity to thank patrons for using the History Center collection and to make sure businesses have properly credited the Center. When they haven't given credit, it is almost always an oversight. Staff gently reminds them that they had agreed to do so and ask if they would like the Society to provide them with preprinted credit lines. Those are available in different sizes and shapes. Keeping positive news of the History Center circulating is essential to attracting new volunteers.

In summer 2008 the History Center initiated an internship program through the local community college. The History Center pays tuition for two elective credits (approximately $150), and receives sixty hours of work from each intern. Such internships are a great way to get vital work done and to increase the involvement of young people in local history activities. If you are interested in setting up internships, contact your area's closest educational institution. Northwestern Michigan Community College in Traverse City already had a Service Learning system set up, and the History Center simply tapped into that system.

Volunteer Retainment

Once volunteers are drawn to an organization, it is essential to maintain their enthusiasm. The method varies from institution to institution, depending on the nature of its volunteer corps. At the History Center, morale depends on balancing expectations of professional work standards against the maintenance of a relaxed and enjoyable working atmosphere.

Almost all History Center volunteers are retirees. They come from successful careers where professionalism was a daily expectation. They are attracted to an organization that believes a small, local institution can also be professional and well managed. The History Center Board has encouraged the archivist to implement policies consistent with SAA standards. Such high expectations seem to have encouraged the volunteers to be proud of their work and stay with the job.

On the other hand, the History Center is one of the locations for the area's local history community. Volunteers and researchers alike seem to be drawn to its friendly atmosphere. Because of space limitations, volunteers processing collections are often in the same room as researchers. Conversation is allowed and actually encouraged. Often a researcher's question is answered by a volunteer working at the other end of the table.

In keeping with this casual atmosphere, it is extremely important that a lone professional who works with volunteers untrained in archival principles keep his or her ego in check. Archivists certainly have valuable advice to give to their boards and volunteers, but they must realize, and acknowledge, that the street runs both ways. The archivist may understand provenance and original order, but the volunteers also have valuable knowledge. At the History Center, the volunteers are founts of knowledge on local history, area politics, and interpersonal relationships. The professional in this situation does well not to see herself as the "archival boss." Rather he or she is a member of a team that comes together to create a well-functioning institution.

As this team grows, each new volunteer fills out an application form. Initially these help determine what type of project a volunteer might enjoy and have the ability to do. At the History Center about two-thirds of the volunteers work directly under the archivist on collections' processing. The others work on administrative, program, and publication activities that are not the archivist's responsibility. Whatever a volunteer's work may be, it is necessary for someone to actively monitor whether volunteers enjoy their work. If he or she seems dissatisfied, ask about it. These people are volunteering, and if they do not enjoy what they are doing, they will not stay.

Sometimes this means that the tasks being done may not be the most pressing projects calling for attention or the ones the archivist would most like to see get done. The truth is that in a historical repository, most items have waited years for attention. Assuming the storage conditions are minimally suitable, these items can wait a few more years. When a volunteer is available, it is necessary to find something he or she wants to do.

Similarly, when a volunteer appears at the door, he or she should be put to work as soon as possible. Strike while the iron is hot. If you have a willing volunteer, find him or her something to do! People are creatures of habit, so once they are in the habit of volunteering one day a week, for example, then the supervisor can work on moving them on to other tasks that might be more pressing.

Ultimately, successful management of volunteers in a small institution calls for the archivist to be a member of a team. Good volunteers are a valuable and scarce resource and should be treated as such. The success of most small nonprofits, and certainly the success of the History Center, depends on them.

Some colleges host annual internship fairs. Plan to attend (or assign an intern to attend) and distribute brochures. If you are seeking volunteers, talk to colleagues at your institution, post announcements in areas where you feel you might find the most qualified and trustworthy individuals (such as service organizations), and look for volunteer fairs if your area offers such an opportunity.

Have interns or volunteers submit either a resume or an internship application. This can be done through e-mail or regular mail. Then schedule an interview and conduct a face-to-face meeting with the applicant. If the student is from another state, a phone interview may be more convenient. You do not have to accept an intern or volunteer just because he or she applies. Once you have selected the intern or volunteer of your choice, set a start date and time and notify the intern/volunteer and your work associates. Create a folder on each intern/volunteer, by name, and file all relevant forms, information, time sheets, and so on for future use.

If you think that the intern or volunteer is not a good fit for you or your institution, let that person know right away. Be honest about why you think the person is not a good fit. In some cases you may need to talk to the school that runs the internship program. If you were "given" a volunteer by someone within your institution, you may need to discuss the situation with that colleague. Sometimes there is no way around it, and you need to make do with the situation.

On the first day, spend the first hour orienting the intern or volunteer to your institution, his or her work area, supervisors and staff, policies, assignment(s), where to eat, parking, and more. Allow time for questions. Make clear any conditions that would result in dismissal and early termination of the internship (theft, inappropriate behavior, etc.). Advise him or her of any necessary training or reading. Having a formal orientation hour establishes a positive tone for the internship and conveys the message that you are organized, that you plan your time, and that you are prepared. You are a mentor—teach the intern or volunteer good skills.

Monitor your intern or volunteer. Some sponsors like to have weekly meetings with interns to check on their progress and adjust their assignments, as needed.

When the internship or volunteer opportunity ends, conduct an exit interview with each person and have each fill out an evaluation sheet and turn in any keys, equipment, or passes. Acknowledge the end of a student's assignment/ project and accomplishments. Some institutions have farewell lunches or something similar, but it's not necessary. Students or volunteers may ask you for a letter of recommendation. If they do, save these on your computer or at least save hard copies in a file. Interns frequently want recommendations, so make sure you record the dates of the internship and details of the project and work. Now is also the time to fill out any student intern evaluation sheets and place them in the student's file.[8]

Records Management

Creating and sustaining a records management program is essential for all organizations. Whether or not you are in charge of creating, implementing, or maintaining the records management program for your institution will depend on your role. Many archivists in small shops assume by default the role of records manager in addition to their archival duties. Most archives maintain not only their special collections or externally acquired collections but also institutional records. Many smaller institutions do not have a formal records management system in place. Usually departments deposit records whenever they do an office "cleanout," while others never turn over records.

If you are starting an archive, do not assume that your work is done once you have your policies in place for researchers and staff. To have a successful institutional archive, you need to have a successful records management program, so creating a records management policy to handle institutional records may be your next step. Start by reviewing any existing practices:

- Are any of the departments regularly handing over records?

- If so, are those the records they should be turning over to the archives?

- Are they following a regular schedule?

- If so, what is that schedule and how was it set up?

When creating a records management program in a small shop, it is best to start from the top down. You need to gain support from the top levels of your administration. Make the case that by instituting a records management program the institution will save money and protect itself legally. If your institution has a general counsel or a legal consultant, it would be best to consult with him or her throughout the process. That person may also be one of your biggest advocates for creating a program.

A good place to start is by creating a blanket policy that will need the approval of your governing body. This policy should contain the following elements:

- An introduction including the purpose of your policy

- The policy statement

- The scope of the policy

- You and your department's responsibilities

- Definitions or records management terminology

- Retention recommendations

- Any other relevant legislation that might affect a records policy, such as HIPAA (Health Insurance Portability and Accountability Act) or FERPA (Family Educational Rights and Privacy Act)

You may need to include other elements, depending on your institution and the goal of your records management program.

AN ARCHIVIST DOES WHAT?

BY RUSSELL L. GASERO

Do I want to become an archivist? What, exactly, do archivists do? Is it worth the time and energy?

These are the questions that prompted the establishment of an internship program in the Archives of the Reformed Church in America (RCA Archives). *Archivist* is not exactly a household term, and few children stop playing to daydream about being archivists when they grow up. History majors might become familiar with archives if their school is fortunate enough to have one—and if assignments require searching primary sources for papers and other class work.

This state of affairs prompted discussions with a colleague in the history department at one of our denominational colleges, and the idea for an internship to explore those questions was born. It began as a semester-long experimental program designed to help a student determine whether or not this would be a valid career path. It seemed that this would be a helpful process before investing the time and expense of another year of graduate education only to discover that this was not a good fit as a career.

An internship in this program carried a different connotation than most. To explore the full nature of archival work, the internship was started on a professional level. The student was required to be in residence for a semester in New Brunswick and to work full-time in the RCA Archives while undertaking a rigorous reading course in archival theory and the history of the Reformed Church in America.

Entering the internship with no sense of what archival work involved meant the student would spend a significant amount of time at the beginning reading and learning while engaging in some basic archival tasks. The readings involved Greg Hunter's *Developing and Maintaining Practical Archives: A How-to-Do-It Manual,* some of the titles in the SAA's Basic Manual Series, and readings from the *American Archivist* and other sources.

Many institutions are developing records management programs because of laws related to privacy and corporate record keeping, such as Sarbanes-Oxley. When crafting your policy, consider establishing a committee of stakeholders to work with you to cover the most important elements. You may want to include someone from information technology, the general counsel's office, department heads, and any other stakeholders that you feel may be important contributors. Figure 1 is an example of a comprehensive records management policy developed by a records management committee at Wellesley College.

Once your blanket policy is in place, notify all departments that you are embarking on a records management program. You will need to make a contact in each department of your institution. A more formal option is to assign someone from each department to handle the records within that department,

Each day, the intern would engage in conversation about the readings and maintain a personal journal of reactions, questions, and reflections. The conversations would offer supplemental information to the readings and real-world examples from the RCA Archives work.

After discussions with the school's faculty, it was determined that for the program to qualify for a full semester of credit, it would have to be rigorous. There would be minimal "gofer" assignments. The intern would engage in the work at the same level as a professional just entering the field. It was also decided that the work would be on a pass/fail basis—the only way to fail would be to not show up or to skimp on work. If the student did not enjoy engaging in the work, it would be apparent that this would be a poor career choice for him or her, and a different assignment would be created that could engage his or her talents and interests.

If the student determined that a career in archives was not an appropriate path, the internship experience would still be considered a success. The internship pushed the student to develop new skills and interests and to engage in significant self-reflection about careers in the field of history and information and records management. It created an opportunity to explore the professional nature of the archives as well as to grow intellectually and to mature as a young adult.

The end result for the student was a semester's worth of credit and a good letter of recommendation for his or her credential file. The letter would be one that attested to the student's sense of responsibility and ability to engage in self-directed work and to work with minimal direction—a letter attesting to his or her work ethic and accomplishments, not necessarily just preparation for a position in another archives.

Since the program started in 1999, two interns have become directors of libraries, two have become museum professionals, and one is now working in an archives. In 2009 the internship was tried as a summer internship. While meaningful for the student, it did not provide enough time for an intern to fully engage the literature and be able to undertake serious work in arrangement and description. The summer option is a viable option but will need some changes to make it more practical for a student with minimal background.

It was clear that the result of a semester of hard work and an opportunity to change roles from student to working professional enabled the intern to adequately answer the questions, "Do I want to become an archivist?" and, "What, exactly, do archivists do?"

including organization, retention, destruction, or transfer to the archives. The people who handle these responsibilities may be called departmental records officers or coordinators (DROs or DRCs). If you go this route, plan to meet with your human resources department to talk about this responsibility being written into the job description rather than being assigned to a specific person. Then any new person in that position will know that he or she is to serve as the DRO or DRC for that department.

Once you know what you'd like to do, consider writing an implementation plan. You can share the plan with your institution and stakeholders, but it is most important for you. The implementation plan should include your current situation, desired outcomes, what steps you need to achieve those outcomes, and, finally, a rough timetable. This document will serve as a series of steps to

FIGURE 1 **WELLESLEY COLLEGE RECORDS MANAGEMENT POLICY**

Records Management Policy, approved by Board of Trustees April 11, 2008

Introduction and Purpose

Records created by Wellesley College staff and by faculty in their administrative roles as they work to fulfill the College's educational mission are essential to the efficient operation of the College, to preserve the College's history, and, in some circumstances are subject to legal requirements. Proper management of such records is therefore necessary.

The purpose of this document is to:

- establish a records management policy for Wellesley College;

- define key concepts specific to the Wellesley College policy; and

- describe a framework for implementing this policy through a records management program.

Policy Statement

Wellesley College is committed to meeting its administrative, fiscal, legal, and historical obligations by systematically managing the records created in the course of the College's academic and administrative operations. The management of records includes appropriate practices for organizing those records, effective archiving of those records determined to have permanent or enduring value, and proper destruction of those records deemed to have no permanent or enduring value once operational needs have been met and no legal considerations require retention.

Implementation of this policy will assist Wellesley College in meeting its operational and legal obligations and in preserving its historical record. Further, the College will benefit from the increased organizational efficiency that implementation of this policy will provide. This policy and relevant materials developed as part of the records management program will be made available to the Wellesley College community for their ongoing reference.

Scope

This policy applies to all records created at Wellesley College during the course of its educational and other activities. Records created by employees of Wellesley College in the normal course of business, and by faculty in their administrative roles, are the property of Wellesley College.

Authority and Responsibilities

The President, Officers, and senior administrative staff of the College are responsible for communicating this policy to College employees and have general oversight of this policy.

The Records Management Officer is responsible for developing and administering a records management program for the College, and will help employees understand how to implement that program.

All employees of Wellesley College are responsible for managing and maintaining the records they create in compliance with this policy and the records management program developed by the College.

Definition of "Records"

Records are "information created, received, and maintained as evidence and information by an organization or person, in pursuance of legal obligations or in the transaction of business." (ISO 15489-1:2001(E) Information and Documentation – Records Management Part 1: General, 3.15) Records are defined by content rather than by format. Records include those that are hard copy, electronic (including Web pages), or any other format from which information can be retrieved.

Records include but are not limited to official College publications, fiscal data, official correspondence (including electronic correspondence), minutes of meetings, reports, and student and employee files. For the purposes of this policy, records are defined broadly to encourage consideration of the appropriate use and retention of all information created in the course of business.

Critical Records

"Critical records" are those records determined to contain essential information needed for operational continuity following a catastrophic event. The Records Management Officer will work with others at the College to determine which records are to be considered "critical records," and to develop procedures that protect them and make them accessible and useable after such an event.

Preserving or Disposing of Official College Records

The Records Management Officer, in consultation with the College's legal counsel, will work with College offices to develop records retention schedules appropriate to each office's circumstances.

The Archivist is responsible for determining which College records have permanent or enduring value. Records deemed to be of permanent or enduring value will be transferred to the Wellesley College Archives on a regular basis. Electronic records of permanent or enduring value will be archived in a way that appears best to allow future accessibility of their content. Routine data backup is not a substitute for the archiving of electronic records that have permanent or enduring value.

Records deemed to have no permanent or enduring value will be retained according to records retention schedules, and properly disposed of as described in those schedules once the retention period has ended.

(cont.)

achieve your ultimate goal. The timetable should include a realistic timeframe to achieve the work that needs to be done.

With your plan in writing, work with the departments to establish your departmental contacts. Set up meetings with every department to discuss the records that are created and maintained by those departments. Create a survey form to capture the information gathered during the interview and to draw up a list of these record groups based on applicable federal, state, and local laws. Also consider the records' value within your own institution and any relevant institutional policies. Consult other sources, such as records policies from similar institutions, Internet sources, and books such as Donald Skupsky's *Recordkeeping Requirements* or *Records Retention Procedures,* as necessary. (See Appendix A for publication information.) If you have some funding, there are several software programs that can help you schedule records, such as Zasio[9] or Retention Manager 3,[10] to name a few. If you have access to legal counsel or your institution has a general counsel's office, have that office review and approve any schedules to avoid future legal problems related to your records management program.

In addition to creating the policies and setting the schedules for each department, you also need to find ways to organize, store, and track these records. Large record facilities have boxes barcoded and tracked using various software systems. You should not expect to re-create this process with a one-person operation. Instead, create or borrow basic forms and adapt them to fit your needs. *Sample Forms for Archival & Records Management Programs,* a book published by the SAA and ARMA International, is a good place to find the forms you will need. (See Appendix A for publication information.) Create standard box labels for each department to use so you can easily identify the following:

- What is in a box

- Which department generated it

- When it was sent to archives

- When it should be destroyed

KEY TERMS }

A **retention schedule**, which may also be known as a disposal schedule, records schedule, records retention schedule, or transfer schedule as defined by Richard Pearce-Moses, is "A document that identifies and describes an organization's records, usually at the series level, provides instructions for the disposition of records throughout their life cycle. Retention schedules may also include instructions for the disposition of documents and other materials that are not official records."[11]

To locate and determine when an item should be destroyed, create color-coded stickers with the destruction date and place them on each box in the same location on that box so that you can read and pull them. These stickers should be on the same side of the box as the box labels so that you know what it is that is being destroyed. When it is time to destroy materials, notify the generating department that the materials will be destroyed. In some cases, the materials may have a litigation hold on them and cannot be destroyed until that hold is lifted.

You will also want to create procedure documents for departments to follow once their records have been surveyed and scheduled. These documents should include:

- Department-specific guidelines for handling and storage of paper and electronic records (this is in addition to the department-specific schedule)

- Guidelines for sending materials to the archives

- Procedure for managing and transfering electronic documents

- Procedures for sending inactive materials to an off-site vendor or a records storage facility

- Procedures for properly destroying records

- Any forms you have created to facilitate records management

You may find that other documents are needed to assist departments in properly storing, transferring, and destroying records. These documents should be accessible to the record creators and managers within the departments. Place all of these documents in one location, such as your website, interoffice wiki, or intranet. By making all of these documents accessible electronically, you can easily update the documents and have them available for departments to do a "one-stop-shop" for all of the records management information they may need to do the job.

Electronic Records Management

When creating and enforcing records schedules, electronic records should not be treated any differently than paper records. What will be different is the storage and destruction of electronic records. If you have an Information Technology (IT) department, work closely with the head of that department or whomever he or she assigns to work on this project with you. If you are unable to partner with IT, you may need to go back to your governing body or legal counsel to discuss your options for dealing with electronic records that are out of your control. If all else fails, when you get requests for information held in electronic form, send the patron to the IT department. Eventually they may decide that it is not appropriate for them to be the "gatekeepers" of electronic records and a solution may come to fruition.

{ **KEY TERMS**

Disposition or final disposition of records is defined by Richard Pearce-Moses as "Materials' final destruction or transfer to an archives as determined by their appraisal. Records may be transferred to archives in their entirety, or in part by sampling or selection."[12]

CREATING A RECORDS MANAGEMENT PROGRAM AT ILLINOIS WESLEYAN UNIVERSITY

BY MEG MINER

Illinois Wesleyan University is a liberal arts university, founded in 1850, with an enrollment of 2,100. Periodically since our founding, people holding positions within the university have also assumed the duties of archivist. It wasn't until 2000 that a professional archivist was employed for that purpose. This is a tenure line position reporting to the university librarian and has responsibilities that include academic librarianship roles (such as reference, collection development, and bibliographic instruction). Therefore, less than 20 percent of time each week can be devoted to departmental needs. There are no employment possibilities for professional staff to assist the archivist, but the library does employ work-study students and the archives is allowed 5.5 of these positions, amounting to 55 hours a week of undergraduate student labor.

When I was assigned to an interim archivist position in 2005, within a few years of a major transition across the top administrative levels, I realized that much of the material cleaned out of those offices and sent to the archives for "sorting" was not relevant to the archives' goals as stated in the collection development policy. Conversely, there were gaps in the documentary record of the university because the archives did not receive some material it should have from a number of campus units and committees.

The process of appraising new material and fielding requests to accession material led me to wonder what types of documents other offices retained or destroyed and the decision-making processes used across campus to employ records retention and control. I undertook an informal survey of a few campus units in order to assess the current status of our records' life cycles. Two of the seven offices I visited had formal plans for record retention and disposal: the Business Office (dated 1988) and the President's Office (dated 2002). People I spoke with in other offices expressed a desire for written guidance on what they should keep and what it would be safe to dispose of. Many offices also thought that digital reformatting services would help them do their jobs.

After making these observations, I wrote a white paper on this topic[13] and proposed that the university make a formal declaration of its records retention policy. The purpose of the proposed records retention policy was to provide a written resource for stakeholders to consult in determining whether or not something they have custody of should be kept, destroyed, or transferred to the archives and to provide time intervals for those actions. I hoped that a mutually agreed-upon policy would provide continuity of actions throughout personnel changes as well as alleviate misunderstandings of what could and could not be accessioned to the archives' holdings.

Until the administrative transitions were complete, including a change in the office of the university librarian, this proposal did not gain support. All personnel in administrative levels above and including me were in interim positions. These levels of campus structure settled, but it wasn't until a new university librarian was appointed that the proposal gained momentum.

Following discussions with the provost, the university librarian was able to circulate the white paper among the President's Cabinet. Late in the fall of 2007, I was asked to develop a records management policy that would outline responsibilities and begin providing a framework for record types involved. I created a policy based heavily on a document created by another small institution, Luther College, whose archivist, Rachel Vagts, generously answered my questions about getting this kind of initiative off the ground.

By the end of May 2008, my university librarian and I were invited to the President's Cabinet meeting to answer questions about the policy and discuss the next steps needed to move it forward. We asked that the president send a memo to all campus offices indicating his support for this program and requesting cooperation as I undertook a formal survey of records management practices and needs in each unit. He agreed to do so.

I laid out an ambitious time line for visiting offices on campus to identify particular needs and to get a better sense of the content they produce and/or house. I used conversations with support staff and department heads alike to promote the archives as a service as well as a repository. One misperception was common: many people thought they would never again have access to records they sent to the archives. I assured them they could determine the amount of time their records stayed for an "active life" in their offices and that if they needed something from them after transfer to the archives, we could provide direct access to their staff members or retrieve the needed information.

My time line for this process was not realistic. I thought one academic year would be enough to talk to people and to write up a policy that reflected campus-specific practices and needs. A year and a half into the process, I have only visited approximately 15 percent of our campus and have many conversations to follow up on. I found that most people do not know what laws or professional associations recommend for their types of records, and much of what I need to do is chase down leads for existing guidance and talk through options with the university's legal office.

Many conversations go beyond what is necessary for records management or archives purposes. People say that they would like their processes and daily workflows streamlined and accessible to them digitally from any location twenty-four hours a day, seven days a week. They have not considered the costs of creating digitized documents, are unaware of problems with text recognition and storage/retrieval over time, and do not see the need for applying records life cycles to digital content. At the same time, I am aware that both text and audio/visual digital content creation that is relevant to our history is increasing, and frequently the larger media files are hosted by off-campus members. This reality necessitates a close working relationship with the campus Information Technology office.

The people I speak with at all campus levels have been cooperative and even relieved to discuss their records management needs. From the texts I read in preparation for this project, I thought buy-in would be the hardest part. Instead, focusing my surveys on what's relevant from fiscal, legal, and archival standpoints and following up with recommendations have been the most difficult parts. I am sympathetic to office managers' daily needs, and I feel these talks have been great bridge-building devices between all aspects of campus and the archives, but I have not yet achieved my goal of establishing a campus-wide process for records transfer to the archives. The work continues!

Creating an organized records management system is time-consuming and will not be done overnight. It may take months, or more likely years, to complete, but it should not be ignored. How you go about creating a records management program will depend greatly on the structure and politics of your institution. As you move through this process, electronic records and records in non-paper format should not be left out. Although archivists are traditionally seen as keepers of papers, moving forward we need to remind ourselves and those around us that history is still being created in the electronic world, and if we don't take steps to preserve it, we are consciously deleting an entire chunk of our history.

IT'S WHO AND WHAT YOU KNOW IN MANAGING ELECTRONIC RECORDS

BY TERRY BAXTER

The Multnomah County Records Program has existed since 1977 with either one or two professionals providing both records management and archives services to a county with between 5,000 and 6,000 employees and more than 200 distinct programs. It maintains a full service records center; creates comprehensive retention schedules; takes custody of, describes, and provides access to county archival records; and provides training to county employees on a variety of records related topics.

Until 2003, the records program provided minimal specialized training or guidance to county staff related to electronic records management. In 1998 the county records program started a project to create comprehensive records retention schedules for all county programs. This process was substantially completed by late 2002. But these schedules rarely explicitly referenced electronic records, nor did they provide any specialized guidance for applying the retentions to electronic records.

In 2003, the County Records Program and the Information Technology Division jointly issued guidelines to assist county employees in complying with records management requirements regarding e-mail messages. Even though this document was limited to e-mail and issued as guidance only, it was the first real step in creating an electronic records component in the County Records Program's functions. It also highlights the strategy used by the program to affect change. Rather than attempting to prescribe action through policy or rule, it approached electronic records management as both a customer service and a stakeholder collaboration issue. This can be a very effective strategy for lone arrangers, as they often do not have the organizational clout to force changes.

The most significant change in the approach that the records program takes toward the management of electronic records occurred in late 2003. It is interesting that this change occurred, not as a result of some sort of planning process, but serendipitously.

This is something to keep in mind when approaching electronic records (or any other major policy initiative) in a small shop. "Chance favors the prepared mind" is an old saw, but it is the standard approach to problem solving in the records program. It does *not* involve just sitting around waiting for something to fall into your lap, however. It requires having an informed background about issues, a desire to make connections within your organization, a sense of what you'll get back for the time invested (a "bang to buck" ratio, in the vernacular), and the willingness to take a measured chance when it's offered.

In this case, chance involved a study initiated by one of the county commissioners to assess space needs for the occupants of the Ford Building, including the Records Program. Some of the study task force's early recommendations were clearly untenable that most records could be destroyed because the county was not subject to the public records law; that no one used the facility, therefore no one would notice its closure; or that tens of thousands of cubic feet of records could be scanned and included in a digital imaging system. But some of the other recommendations were more grounded and posed a real threat to the existence of the program. Most of these consisted of either some sort of outsourcing or the return of all record-keeping requirements to the various departments.

The Records Program, which participated as a task force member, saw this as an opportunity both to educate the county commissioners about the role of the Records Program and to initiate a formal effort to provide policy guidance regarding the management of electronic records. The Space Needs Task Force suggested two significant recommendations for the program. The first was the move of the program to new space and the second was the charge to establish an Electronic Records Keeping Committee, which was required to create a "road map" moving the county toward authentic electronic record keeping.

The Electronic Records Keeping Committee met from August 2003 until it issued its final report in June 2004. Its steering committee included representatives of the Records Program, the County Library, and the Information Technology Division; the remaining members were from various county programs from all departments.

The final recommendations of the task force were the following:

- The creation of an Electronic Records Oversight Committee (EROC) with a mission to develop a program to promote and encourage the use of electronic record-keeping systems in county agencies

- The review of existing electronic record-keeping systems with the aim of determining their ability to manage electronic records

- The development of contracting rules that would include electronic records management review of all new systems purchased

These recommendations were nearly dead on arrival. They were certainly not implemented in even a marginal way. But they planted the seeds for what grew into a modest but successful electronic records program. The county currently does the following:

- Accessions electronic archives and short-terms records

- Provides specific guidance toward the retention of electronic records and systems

- Works with the Information Technology Department to assess legacy data and its retention and management needs

- Works with the County Attorney's Office to develop countywide e-mail standards and training

- Is routinely consulted on new electronic records systems, like the county's electronic medical records system, which impact records storage and preservation

So how did a small program get to this point from a non-starting committee report? Through serendipity. The work on the Electronic Records Committee built bonds and trust with key county departments and programs, most notably the Information Technology Division, the County Attorney's Office, and the County Chair's Office. Work done to develop the committee report demonstrated the expertise held by the Records Program and led programs to ask for assistance when dealing with records-related issues.

Small successes, like replacing expensive and hard-to-use electronic reports with a simple scan and film hybrid solution, led country programs to ask for and rely on Records Program expertise. Trust is often built on a series of small successes like this. The current situation is one in which most questions involving digital systems and electronic records have at least some input from the Records Program.

The key to this success in a small program is simple. Understand the issues, be ready when your opportunity knocks, and don't just sit there when it does.

Whether or not you have control over your electronic records, you should make an attempt to prevent the "digital dark age" from falling on your institution. Work with the various departments in your institution to help you capture and preserve the increasing cache of electronic records, and whenever possible keep the records in their electronic form.

If you are your own IT specialist, the task of accessioning, maintaining, and preserving these records may seem daunting, but that is no excuse for letting them go. Many institutions now create their publications and other important documents in electronic form only. If you do not save these documents, you will lose the content. To save your records, you should target the most important electronic records, such as institutional publications and critical documentation. There are various ways of preserving these, from saving them as PDF files to printing them; however, keeping the document in electronic form is preferred if at all possible. How you save your electronic documents will depend largely on your technological capability, your own knowledge, and the limits of your server and network. Lone arrangers are often their own IT department, yet they are not IT professionals.

If you are able to save your records electronically, set up folders to organize your files by department, type of record (such as newsletters or other publications), or however makes most sense for your organization, much in the same way you have been organizing your archives' paper records. You will also want to have a uniform system of naming files to keep them organized, such as chronologically or alphabetically. If you are your own IT department, speak with your supervisor about the possibility of getting a dedicated server specifically for preserving electronic records that are sent to the archives. By keeping a separate, dedicated server, you have a better chance of preventing the files from being corrupted by other users. Try to ensure that there is a backup power supply so that if your building loses power you don't lose your information. You may also be able to add a dedicated server to the bank of servers that your institution maintains.

Consult with departments to understand what records they are creating electronically. Set up basic guidelines for file naming and transferring records to the archives. If records are being created in a database or software system, find out how those systems are set up and how the information is stored and backed up. Talk to your IT department to set up ways to have old information deleted from the system according to the established records schedule and have any archival information transferred as needed. If you are dealing with proprietary software systems, you may need to work with software vendors to find ways of storing and saving essential information.

One of the most difficult aspects of electronic records management is the massive amounts of e-mail that come in and go out of your institution. You will need to consult with IT, department heads, and any legal counsel to determine the approach to take. The general rule of thumb is that the content determines the value of the e-mail. Some institutions have a blanket policy that all e-mail is deleted after a set period of time, usually three to five years. Many institutions do not like these kinds of policies because they feel that some e-mail needs to be retained longer. Another strategy is to capture all outgoing mail only, but this is also flawed as some messages do not need to be kept. Although there is no foolproof way of capturing all of the messages you do want and none of the messages you don't want, you can come up with strategies to define what it is that you want to capture.

The most effective approach may be to train employees to back up and save important messages related to their work. Which messages are saved will depend on the individual as well as his or her function within the institution. The most essential e-mails will be ones that are sent and received by your governing body and senior administration. Target those stakeholders first, and then decide if you need to train any other individuals to capture and save their e-mails. Put procedures in place to transfer e-mail to the archives at an appropriate time.

Conclusion

Establishing basic programs in your archives may be challenging, but they are important for the long-term sustainability of your archival program. By making your constituents and supervisors aware of these issues and their importance, particularly preservation and records management, you can gain continuing support for your archives. Although you may not be able to begin and maintain all of these programs simultaneously, consider which ones you can implement at your archives.

Preservation is essential to the operation of any archive. Whether your materials are paper or electronic, preserving those materials is the main reason for any archives' existence. Establish preservation priorities and plan to incorporate preservation into your daily workflow. Set aside money in your budget to carry out any necessary preservation activities, such as conservation or disaster planning.

Records management is another core function of any archive, particularly institutional archives. If you are the archivist in an institution, it is imperative that you collect records of evidential value to document the history of that institution. Contact the various departments within your institution to discuss what records they should be sending to you and what records should be destroyed. Both paper and electronic records need to be collected and preserved to fulfill the mission of your archive.

Finally, consider using interns, student workers, or volunteers to assist you with your daily activities. Often there are basic projects that can be done by someone other than you, which will allow you to focus on other, more pressing tasks. Talk to local colleges or universities about recruiting interns or seek out volunteers in your community. Their assistance will be invaluable and can serve to build support for your institution within your community.

NOTES

1 Available at http://www.conservation-us.org/.

2 Monique Fischer, "A Short Guide to Film Base Photographic Materials: Identification, Care, and Duplication," NEDCC Preservation Leaflet 5.1, http://www.nedcc.org/resources/leaflets/5Photographs/01ShortGuide.php.

3 Richard Pearce-Moses, *A Glossary of Archival and Records Terminology* (Chicago: Society of American Archivists, 2005), available at http://www.archivists.org/glossary/index.asp.

4 Ibid.

5 Jeannette A. Bastian and Donna Webber, *Archival Internships: A Guide for Faculty, Supervisors, and Students* (Chicago: Society of American Archivists, 2008), 76.

6 Ibid.

7 Darlene Richardson, "Building an Internship Program from Scratch," SAA Annual Conference, Session 103, San Francisco, 2008.

8 Ibid.

9 Available at http://www.zasio.com.

10 Available at http://www.irch.com/Product-Detail.html?de=239&pr=4&pn=Retention_Manager_3.

11 Pearce-Moses, *Glossary*.

12 Ibid.

13 This paper can be downloaded at http://works.bepress.com/meg_miner/1/.

CHAPTER 5

"Where Do I Put All of This Stuff and Keep It Safe?"
Facilities Management and Disaster Planning

Facilities management and disaster planning are essential to the long-term viability of any archive. Maybe you have been charged with starting an archives, or you have just acquired a collection that is essential to your archives but you have no place to put it. Perhaps you have been asked to plan a new facility, or you need to map out the future of your archives. Finding and managing space is always a challenge for lone arrangers. Often our space isn't large enough or isn't conducive to archival work.

Sometimes we find our archives in spaces with the potential for mechanical failures or natural disasters. Even if we have a brand-new space, we may find ourselves in situations we never expected. We need to plan in advance for the possibility of disasters big and small, even if we haven't encountered one so far. Not only do we need to effectively acquire and manage space, we need to plan for the worst.

Space Planning and Management

Periodically you may look at your space and wonder, "How can I fit one more box in here?" or "How can this small space be used more efficiently?" These are important questions, no matter how long you have been on the job: archivists are constantly vying for space and trying to reconfigure it to fit their archives' changing needs.

So, how *do* you make space? Of course, all of this depends on your archives' physical dimensions and surroundings, internal politics, and archival ethics. Before you do anything drastic, assess your situation to see how you can get more "bang for your buck":

- Are some of the boxes on the shelf only half full?

- Could your collections be housed more efficiently?

- Do you need new shelving or a different kind of shelving?

- Are there collections that are outside of your collecting scope?

- If there is no reason to keep collections that are out of your collecting scope, can you deaccession them and send them to a more appropriate repository?

- Are there collections that get little or no use?

- Do you need to keep rarely used collections on-site for any reason?

- Are there materials that don't need to be housed in the archives? Perhaps they would be better suited in an office or library within your institution.

Once you have answered these questions, you will have a better sense of how to organize or reorganize your space. Assessing your space will be an ongoing process. Often you won't be able to answer these questions immediately.

Building a Case for Space

If you have performed an assessment and are still in need of additional space, you may have to make the case for it. If your assessment was prompted by a new acquisition, consider whether or not the acquisition is necessary. Then, before charging into your supervisor's office and demanding more space, build an effective case for *why* you need that space. Consider the following issues:

- What is the cause of your storage problem?

- How much space do you need, not only now, but for future acquisitions?

- What solutions can you offer? (off-site storage, deaccessioning, etc.)

- Do you need two storage spaces to separate collections, such as those containing unstable nitrate film or other vulnerable materials needing special storage conditions, contaminated records (such as moldy papers), or oversized records from your other collections?

It pays to do the math. If you can calculate how much space you need, it will help you determine whether or not that space will be on-site or off-site or if the collection will be split between on- and off-site storage. To start, you will need some measurements. You can get a rough estimate of how much material you already have by measuring boxes or shelving. If you have X number of shelves that are all the same size, you can measure the length of one shelf and then multiply it by the total number of shelves. If you are trying to measure square footage, you need to measure not only the length of the shelves but also the depth. It may be difficult to figure out how much material you have if it isn't shelved or even boxed. You can get a rough estimate by measuring the boxes (if the material is in boxes) and multiplying the box length by width and then multiplying that by the number of boxes. If the box sizes vary wildly, this may be a tedious and time-consuming process. Remember, you can only get an estimate by measuring boxes and shelves, because you can't take the time to consider whether or not those boxes are full.

Once you have calculated the amount of material that your archives currently holds, you need to determine how much you acquire on average in a year or any other set amount of time. When doing this, consider several factors. Will you be taking on more materials after you acquire more space? If so, make sure that you account for that increase. You also need to consider how long you need to make your new space last. If your space will be "temporary"— with no definite date to move it to a more permanent space—plan on that space accommodating at least ten years' worth of new acquisitions plus your current holdings. Even if your space is "permanent," how permanent is it? Usually you can count on the space for approximately twenty to thirty years. It is always best to overestimate in this case.

Whether you are adding shelving to an existing space or reconfiguring a new space, finding affordable shelving can be difficult on a tight budget. If you need to acquire additional shelving, consider looking into discounted or used shelving. Often vendors have extra shelves from someone who ordered incorrectly. There are also vendors who specialize in selling repurposed and used shelving. Finally, you may find that a local library, archive, or museum is preparing to build a new space or move. It doesn't hurt to ask them if you could purchase or take the old shelving off their hands.

If you are considering off-site storage space, think about whether or not it is worth the cost to move materials off-site and pay a rental fee for the space and retrieval costs. If you have less than desirable space on-site, such as a basement, determine if there are materials that you are holding for a finite period of time while freeing up better space for permanent collections. If those materials are scheduled to be destroyed, they might be candidates for the undesirable space. Keep in mind that these materials will still need to be accessible and should be stored safely for the time that they need to be kept. If there are known problems, such as consistent leaking/flooding when it rains or rodent or insect infestations, that space should not be considered for *any* records.

No matter what kind of space you have, you need to evaluate the risks and impact of pests within your facility. If you are part of a larger facility, check to see if there is an ongoing pest management program. The building management may have someone come in on a regular basis to spray or set up traps for various types of pests. Check with the building manager to determine where any chemicals may be sprayed and what types of chemicals are being used to make sure that they do not have a harmful impact on your collections. If there is a known pest problem, regularly monitor and replace traps as necessary and call for pest management when needed.

Assessing the Security of the Collections

A crucial part of your overall facilities management is security for your materials. Archival materials can be housed in a variety of settings from closed stacks to open access within a library or other setting. If the materials under your care are truly unique, it is important to put in place security measures to protect your materials from theft, vandalism, or unintentional damage.

Your location within a building or even within another unit such as an office or library will be one factor in determining your security problems. If you are set apart from a larger unit, it may be a bit easier to "lock down" your collections yet still have them accessible to your patrons. If staff or the public are able to pick up your archival materials and walk out with them, you need to act quickly; identify any unique or valuable materials and put security procedures in place.

This will be challenging, especially if you only work on a part-time or volunteer basis. You may also encounter resistance from your colleagues and patrons as you try to shift the overall culture of the institution. Start by revisiting your access policy (see Chapter 1). As you assess your archives' security issues, fine-tune the policy to address specific measures to keep the collections secure. A strongly worded, enforced access policy is your best tool to gaining control over the collections as well as to changing the overall institutional culture regarding the archives.

As a part of your overall assessment of the situation, review your current space. If you have books or other materials on open shelves, purchase enclosed shelves with locking doors to protect collections from being taken in your absence. If you do not have money to purchase proper shelving to secure your collections, write a grant to fund the purchase. (For more information on grants, see Chapter 7.) Another solution may be to move some of the collections to another room that can be locked and accessed only by you or another trusted staff member in your absence. Security starts with control over your keys and pass codes.

Make sure all materials are within view of you or another staff member. Keeping patrons in sight helps to minimize theft and to deter outright vandalism of materials. It may be difficult to keep an eye on patrons at all times as you have other work to do. If possible, bring your work out to where researchers are to keep an eye on them. Do not hesitate to state your policies up front to researchers and staff regarding sign out/registration procedures, food and drink policies, and any other policies you may have in place to protect your materials. Make it clear that you reserve the right to search someone's bag if you think they have something inside that either belongs with or might compromise your collections.

Another option is to install security cameras to deter theft and vandalism of collections. Security cameras can be placed discreetly and aimed at places where a patron could escape your line of sight. If you choose to go this route, purchase a system that records on a continuous basis so that you can go back and review tapes for days or times that you were not in the archives or for times when you suspect that someone stole from or vandalized collections. Even if you have closed stacks, if you have volunteers or interns who have access to your collections, you may want a security camera system. As required by law, post notices that inform researchers, volunteers, or interns that they are under surveillance.

Planning a New Facility

If you have the ability to plan for a new facility, you have some tough work ahead of you. Maybe your "new" facility is a space that already exists—perhaps as an unused room or a space cluttered with "archival" material that needs to be turned into a proper archival storage area. Take advantage of this opportunity to create the space you want and need.

There are several factors to consider when embarking on the planning and construction of a new facility:

- How much space do you need, now and in the future?

- What kind of space are you planning for (storage space, researcher space, workspace, etc.)?

- Where will this space be located?

- Are you fixing up an existing space or building a new space?

- What is your budget?

- Is this project part of a larger renovation project (for example, part of a library expansion plan or tacked onto new office space)?

When reviewing options for new space, you need to keep in mind some key factors. To accommodate your shelving, you will need a level floor. This seems like a "no brainer," but if you are using existing space, have the architect or the construction team check that the floor is level. If it is not, ask them to level it. Ideally, the space will not have windows. Also, take into consideration the load-bearing capacity of the floor, any pillars or other structural barriers, and the type and height of the ceiling in the space. Other things to consider are the location of restrooms and kitchens, which could pose a water or fire threat. Look for any potentially harmful spaces located near the proposed space and avoid them whenever possible.

When planning for an amount of space, consider that the archives may occupy the same space for up to twenty years or more. You can calculate your space by measuring the volume of your current collection and either guessing how much material you will acquire each year or, if you have them, using hard numbers to calculate the average amount of material you accept during a specified period and multiplying accordingly. If you are planning for more than just storage, consider what other types of space you will need. Consider the following possible space needs:

- For researchers

- For processing

- For interns/volunteers

- For new acquisitions/holding area/receiving/supplies

- For isolating items with mold or pest problems

- For your office

- For exhibition space

For specific and detailed information about planning facilities, you may want to look at *Archival and Special Collections Facilities: Guidelines for Archivists, Librarians, Architects, and Engineers,* edited by Michele F. Pacifico and Thomas P. Wilsted (see Appendix A for publication information).

A general rule of thumb is to always ask for more and expect that you will need to scale back in the negotiation process. It is easier to ask for more and cut items you can live without rather than limit yourself and then lament that you didn't ask for something when you had the chance. In your planning, determine what kinds of storage you need for your collections by asking these questions:

- What kind of shelving do you need?

  o Stationary or compact shelving?

  o Does your facility have the load-bearing capacity to accommodate compact shelving?

- Do you need storage for maps, blueprints, or other oversized items requiring flat storage?

- Do you need storage for framed artwork?

- Do you need storage for clothing/costumes?

- Do you need storage for artifacts?

- Do you need storage for audiovisual materials?

When exploring your options for storing collections, look at all of your choices carefully while keeping in mind how much of each kind of shelving you need for your current and expanding collections. This is an area where you might ask for more up front and cut back later.

One of the most important considerations is not only the space but the environmental conditions within that space. Will you have the opportunity to obtain a dedicated HVAC (heating, ventilation, and air conditioning) system for your collections? If you can get a dedicated system, do you need more than one? You might consider two systems, one for general paper collections and one for photographs/audiovisual materials or other materials that may need special conditions. Here again is something that you should ask for, but you may be able to compromise later in the planning process.

If you are given the opportunity to construct a new space, you need to be prepared and involved from start to finish. There are two types of construction that you may be involved in: a dedicated building or suite for the archives/ library or, more likely, your archives will be constructed as part of another project, and the space that you share may have a very different function from an archives. In both cases make sure that you are involved in the process

KEY TERMS }

Compact shelving also known as compact storage, mobile shelving, mobile aisle shelving, or movable shelving is shelving designed so that rows can be moved next to each other, with no intervening aisle, to provide dense storage. By moving rows together, it is possible to eliminate aisles. An aisle can be created between any two rows as needed. Generally rows are parallel to each other, although they may be on a central pivot. Depending on the system, compact shelving may be moved using a manual crank or an electric motor.[1]

from day one. Put your archives' needs on the table and don't hold back. It is important that you make these needs known and get involved in choosing the architect for the project. Try to choose an architect who has designed and built an archives or library. If the architect designing your new space knows little or nothing about designing an archives, see if his or her architectural firm has worked with a library or archive and try to get one of the architects with that experience to consult on your project.

Before your first meeting with the architect(s), write a brief synopsis of your collections, your needs, and your wishes for your new space. The document should contain information about what you currently have, what works, what doesn't work, and what your needs are moving forward. Include any information about your strategic plan. This should be succinct and get your point across to educate the architect. This document should prompt the architect to inquire further into your needs and open a dialogue between all parties involved in the project.[2] If the architect does not have any experience with libraries or archives, meet with him or her to explain your needs in detail and why you have specific requirements. Follow up with the architect throughout the design and construction process to make sure that any problems are resolved quickly. Once construction begins, visit the construction site frequently and alert the architects or engineers to any problems you discover.

Before construction of this space began, the Pediatric Orthopedic Society of North America (POSNA) had no public space for its archives. This new room now serves as the home of POSNA's archives. The space was previously a large workroom/conference room and was considered a quick and temporary solution after a major renovation of the library was put on hold. *Photograph courtesy of Mary Nelson Peters.*

There are a few other major items to consider when planning a new space. Lighting is very important, both for the collections but also for you and your researchers. Make sure that all lights used in spaces where you will have archival materials give off little UV (ultraviolet) light. If the fixtures will give off UV rays, ask to put filters on the lights. Think about any windows in the space. There should not be any windows in the storage area, but if there are, make sure that they have blackout shades to keep out light. If there are windows in the reading room or other non-storage areas in the archives, request UV blocking shades that let light in but help to minimize damage by sunlight.

Plan for any equipment that you or your researchers may need. If you have a sizable collection of audiovisual materials, you may want to create an area away from the table(s) where researchers may be consulting paper documents. This media station should still be within the sight line of you or other staff to prevent theft or vandalism of media. The station should include any playback equipment that researchers will need to access various media, such as video, audio, or microfilm, with corresponding earphones so other readers will not be disturbed. This area should be adaptable so that you can add playback machines, including computers as necessary. The location should contain plenty of outlets or a power strip to avoid overloading the circuit(s). If you do not have wireless access, you may also need a jack for connecting to the Internet.

In planning the space, review the fire suppression system. There are many options, but your budget or your space will dictate which options are available to you. The type of ceiling and the height of the fire suppression system will impact your shelving height and configuration. After choosing your suppression system, review how it may or may not impact your shelving and adjust your needs accordingly.

Finally, make room for computers, processing collections, and new acquisitions. The amount of space you have available will impact how large these spaces may be or if you will have room for them. If your space is limited, you may need to use the researcher area or table to process collections. You may want to get one large table to accommodate both researchers and processing activities if you don't have the space to create two separate areas. Another option is to use the wall space to build in a counter that could be used for processing collections, allowing the researcher to have

Archivist workroom at the University of Portland. *Photograph courtesy of Robert Antonelli, University of Portland.*

his or her own space rather than a shared space. New acquisitions might be placed in a specific section of the larger storage space rather than a designated space. Computers may be on a "bring your own" basis. In that case, make sure that there are electrical outlets and Internet jacks or wireless available to researchers and interns.

Disaster Planning

Disaster planning is a small undertaking with a big impact. Whether your collections are in a new facility or in a less-than-ideal space, disaster planning could mean the difference between having a collection or not. Often disaster planning doesn't occur until *after* a disaster, be it small or large. Creating and implementing a plan should be considered essential to the safety and well-being of not only your collections but you and others that occupy your space.

Although it will take some work up front, it is worth the effort to have a disaster preparedness plan in place. Involve any and all staff within your own organization or any other staff or personnel available within your building. Disasters can range from a leaky pipe to a flooded building due to a natural disaster. Be prepared by first identifying the risks from weather, location, and general maintenance of your building. Consider the following:

- Are you in an area that is at risk for a natural disaster, such as floods, tornadoes, hurricanes, forest fires, earthquakes, volcanic eruptions, high winds, or heavy snow?

- What other kinds of disasters may occur, such as power outages, sprinkler discharges, fuel or water supply failures, chemical spills, arson, or terrorist attacks?

- Are you located near potentially high-risk areas, such as near a chemical or other hazardous waste site, a potential terrorist target, or routes used for transporting hazardous materials?

- Within your building, are there known problems, such as leaks, electrical hazards, old fire suppression systems, or construction that could cause fire/water problems?

- Are there hazardous materials within your collections, such as unexploded ordnance (bombs, grenades), nitrate film, or other chemicals?

Your disaster plan should address any and all of these concerns.[3]

To make your plan work, assemble a small working group within your institution to write the plan, and invite any affected parties to review it and give feedback. For the plan to work, you must be able to assign specific roles and duties to any staff or volunteers who would be involved in identifying problems and assisting in disaster mitigation. If you have a small staff with no other library professionals, consider working with other archivists or librarians in your area who may be willing to help. Their involvement will help ensure that you will have people working with you who understand the nature of archival materials and may be better at handling them in the aftermath of a disaster.

In addition to the larger written plan, be sure to assemble a brief "cheat sheet" and an emergency list of contacts, including cell phone numbers of people willing to assist in an emergency. Also make sure that the list includes local fire, police, and ambulance numbers. Set up a phone tree with you at the top of the list, ensuring that you will be notified first should anyone report a problem that affects the archives. From there you should contact the next person on the list, and then that person should be responsible for contacting the next, and so

THE CATERPILLAR INC. CORPORATE ARCHIVES

BY NICOLE L. THAXTON

While there had been efforts made since the 1980s to capture key historical information and materials, a formal archives program was not established at Caterpillar Inc. until the late 1990s. At that time, an archival consulting firm was brought in to analyze the situation and lay the framework for a new archive program. Formal acquisition, processing, and reference policies were put into place. The historical materials were moved out of an oversized closet and moved into a room in the basement of the company's world headquarters building. In May 2000, Caterpillar hired its first professional archivist.

The first few years were spent focusing on growing the value of the Corporate Archives to the corporation, determining what materials had been saved and what materials needed to be gathered, processing the existing collection, and promoting the services of the Corporate Archives. After a few years, the Corporate Archives moved out of the basement into a more visible location—in part due to the poor environment and moisture from the office above it. The archives office and processed collection were relocated to a space within the company's business library on the top floor of the headquarters building, where it was more visible and easier for customers to find. The unprocessed collection was moved into a storage area elsewhere in the building. The Corporate Archives quickly outgrew both the office and storage spaces and had continuing issues with temperature, humidity, and moisture.

In fall 2005, a team was formed to examine existing space limitations and environmental problems. The team consisted of key customers, facilities management personnel, the Corporate Archives manager, and the corporate archivist. The team reviewed the existing conditions of the archival spaces, determined the annual average amount of new material acquired, estimated the space needs for the next twenty years, looked at the functional space needs for different archival processes, and reviewed standard environmental specifications and new potential locations. To help educate the non-archives team members about the environmental and facility requirements for an archive, the team visited three other archives facilities in the area—two at public institutions and another corporate archives. Additional considerations included the new location's proximity to the Corporate Archives main customer base—the company's marketing, public communications, and legal divisions. Recognizing that this would be the only opportunity to create a facility that would protect the Caterpillar heritage, the team wanted the facility to reflect the value the company places on its history.

After the team chose a new location and finalized its requirements and recommendations, the business case was presented to upper management, and the request to renovate a space for a new archives facility was approved. Given the space needs and environmental requirements, it was no longer feasible to keep the Corporate Archives in the headquarters building. Instead, the team decided to relocate to a building one mile from the main customer base. By summer 2007, design work began with Caterpillar facilities personnel and an external architect. As the process began, the Corporate Archivist questioned the structural stability of the new space, given the weight of the collection. An inspection by a structural engineer identified significant structural flaws, so plans for this location were abandoned, and the search began for another space.

Although many months had passed since the site selection process, the team's second choice was still available. One of the Caterpillar manufacturing plants was being converted into new office space, and there was a section of empty warehouse space within this building that was large enough for the desired size of the facility and close to a main entrance for easy access for traveling customers. Although this location was fifteen miles from the primary customer base, it provided the flexibility to "build" a building within the main building instead of designing within an existing confined space.

With the passage of time and the change in locations, the team updated its plans and recommendations, which required more construction, greater financial investment, and additional approvals from the executive office. Recognizing the importance of preserving the Caterpillar history, the executive office approved the additional investment.

A new team was formed to take the project forward. That team included a design and construction project manager from the Caterpillar facilities management group, the corporate archivist, and the architectural firm. Design work on the new location began in January 2008. During the next five months, the team worked to design the systems needed to meet the environmental standards and design the functional spaces needed for various archival processes. The corporate archivist worked closely with the architects and regularly reviewed all of the architectural drawings to make sure that even the smallest details, like the location of electrical outlets, had been carefully planned to meet existing and future needs.

The project was put out for bid in July, and construction began that September. As construction got under way, weekly on-site meetings were held to review construction progress and discuss developing issues. The goal was to keep construction on target to meet a January move date. As with any construction project, issues—big and small—did develop, but work progressed, and construction was finished in January 2009. Instead of moving immediately, the team waited several weeks to give the new HVAC system a chance to operate and determine if there were any issues to resolve with the temperature and humidity controls before the collection was moved into its new home.

Ultimately, the Corporate Archives moved from a 640-square-foot office with a separate 1,000-square-foot storage space to a state-of-the-art 7,000-square-foot archive facility with a 2,000-square-foot dedicated mechanical room that houses all of the systems needed to maintain the Corporate Archives facility. The "building-within-a-building" concept provided an opportunity to design a space that would insulate the collection as much as possible from building hazards and natural disasters. For example, the entire Corporate Archives facility and mechanical room are rated to withstand an F4 tornado, and the HVAC system can be switched over to emergency generator power at a moment's notice.

The main Corporate Archives space includes separate display, reference, staff, processing, preservation, and storage areas with enough room to grow for many years to come. As soon as visitors walk inside the new facility, they have the opportunity to view the Caterpillar heritage in a whole new light, and they quickly understand the importance that Caterpillar places on this valuable asset.

on. Before rushing to the scene or starting the calls, be sure that it is safe to do so. Depending on the disaster, you may need to wait a few days before you can get in to assess damages and start recovery efforts.

After you have drafted your plan, make sure that it will work when you do have a disaster. Review the plan every year, and update your checklist of supplies as well as your emergency contact list. Review the plan annually with any staff that may be involved. It is a good refresher course for employees that know about it and serves as a good introduction for any new staff. Keep copies of the plan on shared computer drives and post hard copies in multiple locations. Be sure that key staff members keep a hard copy of the plan at home. An easy way to keep the plan handy is by using PReP, or the Pocket Response Plan devised by the Council of State Archivists, or COSA. The COSA website offers the forms you need to create a pocket-sized plan. COSA also sells packs of Tyvek envelopes to house the plan neatly and securely in your wallet.[4] In addition, local archival organizations often hold workshops on disaster planning; you and other involved staff can attend one to gain other insights into this process. Check with your regional archival organization for more information.[5]

If taking on the task of drafting a plan from scratch is too much work, consider using dPlan Lite,[6] a free online service available to nonprofits that allows you to plug in your institution's information to help you create your plan. The plan was designed by the Northeast Document Conservation Center as a way to make disaster planning easier and to encourage more institutions to develop a plan by providing a comprehensive fill-in-the-blank template. There are two versions of dPlan, "in Depth" and "Lite": the latter is suggested for small institutions with limited staff. It will take a while to complete dPlan Lite, and you may not be able to do it in one sitting, but it is well worth the effort. Before using dPlan, you may want to try the online demo to see if it is right for you.

Another simple tool to use is the "Worksheet for Outlining a Disaster Plan" provided by the Northeast Document Conservation Center.[7] This tool will allow you to draft your own disaster plan, set priorities, and capture essential information that you will need in a disaster. The worksheet also provides you with a checklist of materials that you should keep on hand in case of an emergency.

If you work for a nonprofit organization and need to get additional outside help writing your disaster plan, the National Endowment for the Humanities offers a Preservation Assistance Grant for Small Institutions that can provide the funding to hire professional assistance with disaster planning.[8] You can also use grant money to purchase disaster recovery materials. Organizations such as the Northeast Document Conservation Center and Conservation Center for Art and Historic Artifacts can help you prepare your grant application and set you up with a trained professional who can help you draft a plan.

Once the plan is in place, make sure that you have the supplies needed for rescue and recovery of both people and collections. It is best to put together a checklist of items, such as the one below, to keep on hand at all times:

- Plastic sheeting, tarps or Polyethylene (rolls or sheets)
- Plastic bags (the kind that seal)
- Flashlights (Test them and replace batteries periodically, or use hand crank lights.), light sticks
- Batteries
- First aid kit(s)
- Dust masks
- Fire extinguisher (Check the expiration date on a regular basis and keep more than one on hand to accommodate all of your spaces.)
- Rubber boots
- Shop vacuum (wet/dry)
- Large trash can(s)
- Unprinted newspaper or blotting paper
- Fan(s) and dehumidifier(s)
- Rubber gloves (any kind, but disposable latex-type gloves work best)
- Disposable smock(s)
- Goggles
- Large plastic flatbed hand truck
- Mop(s) and bucket(s)
- Brooms
- Shovel
- Water-absorbing "snakes"
- "Rescubes," or plastic storage and transport boxes/bins
- Record-keeping materials, such as clipboards, paper, forms, markers, pencils, labels, disposable camera
- Scissors and utility knives
- Sealing tape (duct tape)
- Protective eyewear
- Walkie-talkies
- Clothespins
- Clothesline

Wet books placed in a plastic bin as part of a disaster planning exercise. This demonstration, which was produced by the National Snow and Ice Data Center, was created to provide a visual (and olfactory) experience showing the damage that can occur if even a small water event is not managed right away. *Photograph courtesy of Allaina Wallace, National Snow and Ice Data Center, Boulder, CO.*

Review the list periodically and make sure that anything requiring maintenance be tested and serviced and that your supplies are still in stock. Replace fire extinguishers and expired batteries in flashlights annually. Most of the items on this list can be stored on the plastic flatbed cart and in the trash can. If you are unable to assemble your own kit, you can purchase a ready-made kit from an archival supply company, but they don't often include all of the materials listed above. You can find a full checklist through Lyrasis[9] that you can copy so that you can identify the location and quantity of the items on the list.

As part of your disaster plan, include a list of freeze-drying and disaster mitigation vendors. This is particularly important if your institution is prone to flooding, hurricanes, forest fires, or other major natural disasters. Freeze-drying wet materials immediately after a flood or water damage prevents books from growing mold and gives you time to get your facilities back in order. You can then gradually thaw and dry the wet materials to reduce additional damage. Companies such as Belfor, BMS Cat, and Munters can provide freeze-drying trucks, specialized equipment, and experienced help to recover collections immediately after an event. These companies are on call twenty-four hours a day to respond to disasters.

Conclusion

Although concerns about archival facilities may, on the surface, seem to play a relatively minor role in your overall work, their setup, care, and management can have a significant impact on your entire operation. Make sure that your space meets your needs and is suitable for your workflow, your staff or volunteers, the collections, and your patrons. If you determine your space is not suited to your collections, advocate for a new space. If you are given the chance to design and move into a new and improved space, take the opportunity to assess your needs and make sure that those needs are addressed. Work closely with architects, engineers, and designers to make sure that your space will be suitable. Check in regularly to make sure that construction is going as planned, and report any problems immediately.

Whether you are moving into a new space or adapting a current space, be sure to address issues such as security, pest management, lighting, fire suppression, and climate control within that space by setting up policies and contacting the appropriate staff to deal with any problems. Create and regularly review your disaster plan and supplies so that you are prepared for any potential emergencies. Disaster planning is a critical part of your facilities management goals. Write a plan even if it is a brief document that lists emergency contacts, a supply list, and instructions for staff in case of an emergency. Review your plan regularly and maintain supplies on-site in an accessible location. Finally, work with staff, patrons, and colleagues to create and maintain a suitable, safe, and flexible workspace.

NOTES

1 Richard Pearce-Moses, *A Glossary of Archival and Records Terminology* (Chicago: Society of American Archivists, 2005), available at http://www.archivists.org/glossary/index.asp.

2 For more information on planning and designing a new facility, see Thomas P. Wilsted, *Planning New and Remodeled Archival Facilities* (Chicago: Society of American Archivists, 2007).

3 Beth Lindblom Patkus and Karen Motylewski, "Disaster Planning," Northwest Document Conservation Center Preservation Leaflet 3.3, http://www.nedcc.org/resources/leaflets/3Emergency_Management/03DisasterPlanning.php.

4 See http://www.statearchivists.org/prepare/framework/prep.htm.

5 See Appendix B for regional archival organizations and contact information.

6 See http://www.dplan.org.

7 Karen E. Brown, "Designing a Disaster Plan," Northwest Document Conservation Center Preservation Leaflet 3.4, http://www.nedcc.org/resources/leaflets/3Emergency_Management/04DisasterPlanWorksheet.php.

8 Grant information can be found at http://www.neh.gov/grants/guidelines/pag.html. For more information about grants and grant writing, see Chapter 7 of this book.

9 Available at http://www.lyrasis.org/Products%20and%20Services/Digital%20and%20Preservation%20Services/Resources%20and%20Publications/In-house%20Supply%20Checklist.aspx.

10 Pearce-Moses, *Glossary*.

CHAPTER 6

"You Want What?"
Reference and Outreach

Reference is connecting patrons to the information they seek and educating them on how to search for the materials they need to complete their work.

Archivists keep collections with the intention that they will provide historical documentation for people, places, things, and activities. Once they have their collections under control, they want to make them available to the constituents, as the sole purpose is for the materials to be used by researchers, both internal and external. Without the possibility of fielding reference requests, there is little incentive to carry out other archival duties.

Providing access to collections means reaching out to researchers and showing them what the archives has and what the archivist can do for the researcher. Outreach activities make collections visible to constituents and address their need for information. Activities such as exhibits, newsletters, workshops, oral histories, and open houses show constituents what the archives has. As archivists engage in outreach activities, the rate of requests, as well as visibility, increase. This provides an additional workload, which in turn provides additional support from the archives' own institution as well as the larger community.

Managing Reference Requests

Reference requests come in all forms: sometimes they are from people who work within an institution and other times they are received from outside sources. For lone arrangers it is important to distinguish between "reference" and "research." Small-shop archivists often provide research services rather than reference services. What is the difference? Reference is connecting patrons to the information they seek and educating them on how to search for the materials they need to complete their work. Research is finding the records or information for the researcher.

Ongoing backlogs and an inability to make frequent updates to databases or finding aids can mean that researchers aren't equipped to do their own searching. Consequently, archivists are often stuck with having to find the information for the researcher rather than directly pointing them toward resources. You need to balance these requests with your daily workload. Some questions can be answered quickly and others may turn out to be extremely time-consuming. You can take steps to manage requests effectively while keeping pace with your normal workload by creating shortcuts and setting up ways to manage frequent requests.

When working alone, you need to adapt to situations as they arise. That means you will often find yourself skipping the formal reference interview by trying to point a researcher to a particular collection or using past reference questions to answer the query quickly. Depending on how the request comes in, you may have the ability to ask questions up front to narrow the request into something you can work with. There will be other times when a researcher sends an e-mail or leaves a message that you will have to follow up on. Do not let a request go for more than 48 hours (unless, of course, you are out of the office), even if your response is simply an acknowledgement that you received the message.

Fulfill requests to the best of your ability. Sometimes, a researcher may come in and request "everything you have on X." In these cases, you need to ask the researcher to narrow the request by asking him or her "what about X?" or "what time period are you looking for?" Usually the researcher can narrow the request to a more reasonable search; if not, indicate that you cannot help unless he or she can narrow the search. A good example of a request comes from Alison Stankrauff, who writes, "One of my favorite reference requests was helping a family in South Dakota who was working to accurately restore a plow that had belonged to their great-grandfather soon after his immigration to the plains from Germany. They had found that the IU South Bend Archives had a copy of a South Bend Chilled Plow Company catalog, and I was able to send them several scanned pages from the full-color catalog, which helped them to restore their family heirloom accurately. They even sent me pictures after completion of the restoration, which was very gratifying." (See case study on page 102.)

In some cases the researcher's request may be too specific. Then it is okay to let him or her know that you do not have anything that matches the request. If there is a particular topic, person, or event mentioned in the request that relates to something in your collection, offer an alternative solution. For example, if a researcher is looking for a picture of the Empire State Building in 1942 and you have a photograph of the building in 1950, he or she may find that to be an acceptable alternative.

The easiest way to manage reference requests is to be prepared. It may take some time, but in the long run it will help you to work more efficiently. Some of these strategies will also help you with not only reference but outreach efforts. Here are some tools that you can create and use:

- A vertical file: A physical file cabinet of files on specific subjects or items that are often requested or a file of any extensive research that you had to undertake. By keeping these files, you save time in the future and can pull up information quickly. This file should not contain originals, only duplicates on which you can write any information as to the location of the originals. These files can help you answer commonly asked questions or provide easy access to items that are requested frequently, such as lists of award winners, biographical information on influential people in your

{ KEY TERMS

A **reference interview** is a conversation between an archivist and a researcher designed to give the researcher an orientation to the use of the materials, to help the researcher identify relevant holdings, and to ensure that research needs are met. Reference interviews are conducted to ascertain the identity of the researcher, as a security measure; to determine the researcher's information needs and purpose; to guide the researcher to appropriate access tools and relevant sources; to inform the researcher of basic procedures and limitations on access, handling of documents, and reproduction; and, after research has been completed, to evaluate the success of the visit and the effectiveness of the reference service offered. The initial reference interview is often referred to as an *orientation interview* or the *entrance interview*. The interview at the end of a research visit is often referred to as an *exit interview*.[1]

organization, and so on. If you have extensive files, a searchable database, spreadsheet, or some other means may help you find things in a pinch.

- Fact sheets: This is essentially a Frequently Asked Questions sheet or Web page that will help reduce the number of requests for common questions. If it is online, you can easily respond to e-mail requests with the link and offer these questions and answers in conjunction with any social media you may be using.

- Lists: Keep simple lists of award winners, board members, presidents, buildings, chancellors, honorary degrees, commencement speakers, major donors, famous members or alumni, institutional name changes, and key events in the organization's history, and update them as necessary. You can easily e-mail or post these lists as needed.

- Time lines: This can be a simple list or, if it is warranted, something as complex as an interactive website. A time line can answer basic questions about major events in your institution's history.

- Citation information: It is useful to establish a standardized citation for both serious researchers and for publications. For researchers citing a document, photograph, or object from your collections, have them include basic information such as container number, folder number/name, collection title, institution name, city, and state (or city, province, country). For publications reproducing materials from your archives, the same citation should be used. For any other publications (such as a newspaper article about your archives or materials in your archives) make sure that your institution and location are properly cited, such as "Courtesy of the X archives, Your City, Your State." In some cases you may request that the researcher provide you with a copy of the final work.

To get a better understanding of your clientele and their needs, track your constituents and their requests. You can then find ways to streamline your reference activities. Something simple such as a spreadsheet or database will do the trick. If you are trying to track general usage, put together a spreadsheet that lists the type of constituent (students, staff, board members, etc.) and the type of request (photographs, books, general history questions). You can track the information for a month or for years. If you want more detailed information about your constituents, track names, contact info (phone or e-mail), the type of request, the collections consulted, whether or not the request was fulfilled, and any other notes about the query. This information can also be helpful in creating or rethinking your collection policy as well as reappraisal of collections.

Nothing will prepare you more than having easy access to box lists, finding aids, control files, acquisition records, or other means of tracking what collections you have and what is in each collection. This will cut down on the time spent per request. Working in small shops often means that we don't have the luxury of having more than a few high-traffic collections described and accessible. Most of us end up searching through boxes using our institutional memory rather than using finding aids. If you have high-use collections, create a box list or index of the materials within the collection to make it easily accessible.

As you settle into your role, you will discover that there are high-use items such as photographs, books, documents, publications, or other individual items. Place these collections in an easily accessible location. If you scan items (whether it is for a patron, an exhibit, or some other use), scan the item as a high-resolution TIFF file and keep a master file on your computer or server. Be sure to properly label any scanned items and organize them into a folder so that they are easily accessible. If you do a lot of scanning, create a database or an indexing system so that you can easily find scanned items in the future. You can always make an image smaller but you can never make it bigger, so if you get a request for an image that doesn't need to be very large, you can scale down the image and turn it into another format, such as a JPEG or GIF. This will be much quicker and easier on your collections if you don't have to scan the item over and over. If you are scanning multiple pages of a text, scan it into a PDF file.

If you don't have scanning equipment or the software to create these digital files, you can create photocopies. In some cases, you may have the opportunity to outsource scanning. If you do outsource, make sure that you get both high-resolution files along with any derived files that you need for your project. You may find that demand for scanned items will warrant the purchase of a scanner and software.

Internal versus External Requests

Handling reference requests for internal constituents may be quite different from handling requests from outside researchers. You may choose not to make a distinction. How much time you spend on an internal versus external request and how thorough you are will depend greatly on what your institution has charged you to do.

If you are struggling with how to deal with internal versus external requests and how much time you spend on either, set up a system to determine a reasonable amount of time to spend on any given request. For example, if the request comes from the president or board of your institution, you may need to do an exhaustive search, especially if the outcome could have an impact on you or your archives. When working with an external researcher, limit the time by searching for a set amount of time or by checking only the most obvious places. If you find that people not affiliated with your institution are putting frequent demands on your time, you may want to set up a fee schedule and charge these researchers for the time spent on a particular request. You can structure the fee schedule in many ways, but one simple way is to state that you will spend 30 minutes on a request and after that researchers will have to pay a set amount per every additional 30 minutes. Adjust the time frame as well as the fees as needed. If your institution sees mostly external researchers, your governing body might find this strategy unacceptable.

A researcher consulting materials at the Emerson College Archives, Boston, Massachusetts. *Photograph courtesy of Angela Lembke.*

A fee schedule can reduce frivolous research requests, but, more importantly, fees can be used to recoup costs or allow you to have a little extra cash on hand to work on an exhibit or fix the copy machine. Different institutions operate under a variety of financial structures, so make sure to get approval before putting a fee schedule in place. You may also need to set up a system with your accounts payable office to determine what type of payment can be accepted and how that money will be allocated within your budget. For information on how much to charge for your services, look at what similar institutions are charging for services.

Following are some services for which you may want to charge:

- Digital reproduction(s)
- Photocopies
- Vital records or genealogical records
- Document certification
- Postage
- Extra copies of old institutional publications
- Audio or video reproduction

A quick search of fee schedules will show that the prices charged by institutions range from nominal to exorbitant. Determine the fee schedule that is most reasonable to your situation.

In the case of internal requests, determine how much time you should reasonably spend on any given request. Some requests may be simple, but others may be much more involved and require searching over a period of time. Depending on what other projects you may be involved in, determine what requires more of your time and minimize any time spent on unreasonable or overly complicated requests. Encourage your constituents to come into the archives and do their own research rather than rely on you to do the research for them. Only you can decide what is unreasonable and what limits you need to set on any given request.

Besides setting time limits on a request, you also need to decide whether or not you *can* fulfill a request. As archivists, it is in our nature to fulfill every request to the best of our ability. However, some requests may need to go unfulfilled due to privacy and other legal restrictions on records. Archivists have a duty to protect the rights of the creators of records. Chapter 2 discussed the importance of having a deed of gift for newly acquired collections. In some cases the donor may request that the collection or parts of the collection remain closed for a certain amount of time. If you are the custodian of administrative records, you need to create your own internal policies for who has access to which records. Access to items such as financial records, employee or student records, or board of trustees' or presidents' records may need to be restricted to only those departments or entities that created the records for a given amount of time.

The type of institution you work for and the laws or bylaws regulating your institution will influence if and how long the records in your archives stay closed. Private institutions or corporations are often not obligated to open their records to the public. It is up to your institution to disclose its records at will. Government and public institutions are usually required to open records either through a Freedom of Information Act (FOIA) request or simply after a certain amount of time has passed, as dictated by law.

You may find it necessary to educate and encourage record creators and donors to think about creation, preservation, accessibility, and use of their records once they are no longer needed and deposited into the archives. Often the creators or donors are only invested in the current needs of the records but forget about accessibility after the materials have reached the end of their immediate use. Creators most likely have not considered whether, when, and to whom a record should be accessible. As discussed in Chapter 1, your access policy should follow any and all applicable federal, state, and local laws, as well as any institutional policies; the document will help you inform donors and records creators as to what will be accessible to whom. In some cases, you may need to redact information in your archives if documents and materials contain personal information, such as social security numbers, addresses, phone numbers, or other identifying information that might be used for criminal activity.

Another reason you may not be able to fulfill a request is that some items in your collection may be too fragile for handling. In some cases a reproduction or a scan can be made to serve as a reference copy, but in other cases, you may not have the funding or the resources to provide even a copy to the researcher. If you find yourself in this situation, explain to the researcher the reasons why he or she cannot have access to the material. If you can, sit with the researcher and make sure that you are the only one to handle the item or take a photograph

REFERENCE AND OUTREACH

BY ALISON STANKRAUFF

Indiana University (IU) South Bend is a small "regional" campus in the Indiana University system. The campus has about 78,000 students, who in large part come from the surrounding urban and rural communities, with a fairly sizeable international student population. IU South Bend has a strong commitment to both serving and working with the community.

I have been the archivist at IU South Bend since 2004. Before that, there had not been an archivist in the position since 1994. The dean of the library had successfully lobbied the university for the creation of my position after a campus accreditation, when the importance of being able to locate and to retrieve appropriate campus documents became apparent. Another key push for the creation of the job was to extend the mission of the campus and have the archives work with the communities that it serves—both the campus community as well as the community beyond—and to document and make accessible archival records.

Reference has been a key part of building the IU South Bend archives. It has also proven to be a core component in sustaining the ongoing work of the archives.

One of the first steps in the process of developing the archives was to establish a Web presence. The archives' website was inaugurated a few months after I began working. The website that was created for the archives was loaded with several key components—mission statement, collection development policy, records management policies, and a number of finding aids. It might be noted, as with many "latent" archives, that I had inherited the archives with no policies. Therefore, creation of all of the basic policies that appeared on the website were of immediate importance in my first months' work. As I've processed more collections, more finding aids have been loaded onto the website. I have also created informational pages, such as the history of the buildings on campus, peace and antiwar activity on campus, the history of the black student union, club and varsity sports history, and so on. I've also made an effort to put up the finding aids that pertain to our community-related collections, such as those from local area industries (collected by a faculty member in our Labor Studies Department), as well as those from notable local figures, such as a suffragette and women's rights advocate.

I have also worked with the library's Cataloging Department to make much of the archives' holdings searchable in the library's catalog. All of our Special Collections books and student dissertations are now cataloged, and the archives' audiovisual materials, including student recitals, lectures on campus, concerts, and theater productions, have also been entered into the library's catalog. I have found that many requests for materials have come from searches in the library's catalog for a variety of different archival materials.

Once the archives had a Web presence, reference statistics went up fourfold from previous months. Requests have rolled in from as far away as India, Germany, and England, as well as many of the states, which I attribute to the fact that the Web-based content is keyword searchable. Very importantly, the website has also served as a resource and point of reference for people in the immediate area and across the state of Indiana, again extending the mission of our campus to reach out and serve the community in which our campus resides.

Another key component of building reference service has been my outreach to the campus community. I have made a real push to get out to campus events and be very active in campus life. It helps my visibility and just helps people know who I am. I get to meet people who make the records that the archives wants to preserve, including the administrators, the administrative assistants, professors, staff, and students. I try to attend each first-of-the-semester event, where all of the student clubs are represented. I make sure to meet and greet all of the current student leaders and let them know about the archives and that we're a resource and that we want to help them maintain their records. I have also appeared at the academic cabinet, which includes all of the campus's deans, to both promote the archives and ask those same deans to speak with their respective departments about the archives. Ever since, I have fielded several requests each year to assist the work of these departments.

Reference is one of the most enjoyable parts of my job as an archivist. I love to connect people with the materials in the archives, and I love the absolute variety of materials that people want information about, access to, or copies of. It's also gratifying to serve a varied set of people. I am always delighted when I know that I have helped people complete their research, finish work on a project, or ferret out information on some obscure event. Reference is the connection between the people and the materials in archives.

as proof of the condition. Researchers will often be understanding, especially if they can see that the item should not be handled.[2]

Internal Advocacy and Outreach

Archival materials can be used for both internal and external purposes. Internal advocacy is a way of using materials to generate interest among your internal constituents. Outreach is a way of promoting your archives to a larger, more public audience. There are advantages and disadvantages to both. In some cases, you may not be able to perform any outreach with a larger public audience.

Both internal advocacy and outreach efforts will help boost your visibility. This, however, can also be a double-edged sword. When taking on any kind of outreach task, consider the work involved and the additional work it may create for you. In many cases, creating visibility is a benefit to both you and your institution because it allows you to connect with your constituents, which in turn keeps your work relevant.

One distinct advantage of both outreach and internal advocacy is connecting potential donors and existing donors to your collections. By promoting your archives through activities, exhibits, and other efforts, you bring the archives to the people. When people are engaged, they can gain a better understanding of your work, which will assist you in fundraising activities and in acquiring collections. The more creative you are in your internal advocacy and outreach efforts, the more engaged your audience will be.

Using Archival Materials for Internal Advocacy

Audience. There may be times when it benefits you to use archival materials to hook an internal audience, such as your governing body, staff, members, faculty, students, or alumni. Depending on your mission, you may be required to reach out to your internal constituents by making them aware of the collections they have at their disposal. In some cases, your archives may only exist for internal purposes.

You can reach out to your internal constituents through presentations, exhibits, workshops, websites, and social media. Presentations can be small workshops, new employee orientations, slideshows for groups of alumni, longtime members, governing bodies, or for special events. Look for opportunities to provide information to both internal and external constituents. If your institution has regularly scheduled events, see if there is a way to become involved in the event or to enhance your involvement.

Look for opportunities to provide information to both internal and external constituents.

When working with an internal constituency only, it is important to show your worth, both from a historical standpoint as well as a practical standpoint. It is likely that you not only serve as the memory of the institution, but that you are the records manager of the institution as well. Even if your institution doesn't have a formal records policy or records manager, you are still involved in the basic life cycle of its records. Reaching out and educating your constituents is an important part of your job. Simple things like brochures and Web pages that assist people in their jobs can make their work more efficient and your job easier. Set up meetings or workshops to help departments manage their physical and digital records and give them information on how to turn over records to the archives and what kinds of records they should or should not send. Often people assume incorrectly that a record is not archival or has no permanent value. They may also assume the opposite and keep records that have no long-term value to the institution.[3]

Besides helping departments operate more efficiently, you can give brief presentations on the history of your institution. It may be useful to give a presentation during a new employee orientation session or to your public affairs or marketing departments. If your organization does not have a public affairs or marketing office, make a presentation to your governing body showing them the resources you have available to them. They may not realize what the archives holds, and you may be able to inspire marketing and fundraising activities that will help your organization grow and thrive.

Exhibits. Both physical and virtual exhibits are an excellent way to reach out to your internal and external constituents. By creating even simple exhibits, you bring positive visibility to your organization. Creating exhibits may be required as part of your job, or they may be an extracurricular activity. They can be simple or complex, involve only you and your resources, or be created by an outside vendor. Your ability to create exhibits will depend largely on a few key factors:

- Time: How much time do you have to commit to creating an exhibit?

- Funding: What is your budget and what can you do with that budget?

- Politics: Do you need to clear what is to be exhibited with someone in your institution?

- Secure display cases: Do you have any, and if so what size and how many?

- No display cases: Can you create reproductions or collages to put on display rather than leaving originals out unprotected?

- Engaging your viewers/visitors: What items will the audience find interesting or eye-catching?

Let's examine each of these factors.

The amount of time you have to spend on an exhibit will be determined by your schedule or dictated by someone within your institution. Remember to manage your time appropriately so that you can create an exhibit while also juggling your regular duties. Exhibits are often accompanied by deadlines. If someone in your institution has asked for an exhibit, make sure that his or her time line and expectations are reasonable. Most people are unaware of the amount of time and effort involved in creating and mounting an exhibit. Even small exhibits can take sixty to a hundred hours, especially if you are doing all of the work yourself. Explain why you might not be able to meet what you consider to be unreasonable expectations. Consider the amount of time it will take you to do any or all of the following: gather materials, create labels, design labels, print/mount labels, work with an outside consultant (if necessary), and create reproductions of materials.

If you need to hire a conservator, exhibit designer, or other consultants for the project, take into account the time it will take to find the right person and the right price and any time it will take to go through multiple designs until you find one that suits your needs. Often, institutions are willing to put forth the time and effort to hire a consultant if they are preparing for a big event such as an anniversary celebration or looking to put up a permanent display in a new or renovated building. If you know of an upcoming event, plan ahead, as it may take a year or more to complete the project.

A major consideration when planning and preparing exhibits is your budget. Do you have a budget for your exhibit? What is that budget and what can you accomplish with that budget? If you are creating an exhibit for a one-time event such as a centennial or other anniversary, you may need or be given a larger budget to hire an outside consultant to assist in creating a more professional exhibit. When creating a physical exhibit, design one that you can reuse in the future. That, however, may not be a possibility, depending on the parameters of what you are putting on display.

If you are not given the opportunity to hire an outside consultant to help you, you can create an exhibit on a shoestring budget with the following materials, which are available at your local art supply store, craft store, or online:

- Foam core board and/or mat board

- Rolling trimmer. If you cannot afford one, you can purchase the following instead.

    o Exacto® knives (box cutter-type or penknife-sized)

    o Self-healing mat

    o Straight edge (T-square, yardstick, ruler—these should be metal)

- Color printer or access to one

- Spray glue (Use this only in a well-ventilated area away from archival materials, as it will spread around the area where it is sprayed.) or glue stick

- Burnishing roller

With these tools at your fingertips, you can create professional-looking exhibits without added expense.

Although the exhibit may not cost much in materials, it will cost more of your time. If you are doing this as part of a paying job, figure out how much you make per hour and multiply that by how much time it will take to research and find materials; write text and labels; print, cut, and mount labels and reproductions; and install. Even a small display can take several hours to complete. If you are expected to do a large-scale display, particularly a permanent display, encourage your boss or governing body to consider hiring a professional exhibit designer.

The most important factor in exhibit planning is your audience and what you are trying to convey. Make your display effective by keeping the following in mind:

- Exhibit content

    o Are the items visually interesting?

    o Do they tell a story?

    o How are the items related?

- Exhibit title

    o Does it need a title?

    o If so, is it catchy or interesting?

    o Will visitors understand the meaning of the title?

    o How will the title be displayed?

        - A banner?

        - Introductory text panel?

- Introductory text
  - Will there be an introductory label?
  - Match the graphic design of the introductory text panel to any item labels.
- Labels
  - Keep text and labels concise—less is more
  - What is the size of your text? It should be at least 18-point type.
  - What is the style of the text? Fancy fonts may be difficult for some patrons to read.
  - Is the design visually appealing?
  - Is the color scheme or design appealing/appropriate/complementary and easy to read?

Overall, the more creative your exhibit, the more engaged your visitors will be.

At the outset, you need to choose a theme. This may take some trial and error before you find items that are interesting, stable enough for display, and plentiful enough to fill out a case and tell your story. If you are having trouble developing a theme for an exhibit, think about how your historical materials might relate to a current event, such as an upcoming celebration. Even if it isn't an anniversary year for the event, you can do a display on what your institution was like 25, 50, or 100 years ago. Look for anniversaries to celebrate, such as the creation of a program, a publication, or other major event. Other possibilities are related materials that you can unite around a common theme, such as famous people at your institution, sporting events, how cultural activities or holidays have been celebrated, or how something was done in the past (cooking, farming, transportation, parenting, etc.).

Now that you have a theme, you need to consider where you are going to mount the exhibit. Will it be displayed in a case or on an open surface like a table or bookshelf? You need to decide what you are putting on display. If you intend to display any originals, they should be in a locked case with limited access (preferably, you will be the only person who has access to the case). You also need to consider any microclimates in the cases that may cause damage to originals, such as excess light, heat, or humidity. For open displays you must anticipate the potential for theft or vandalism. These factors, along with the amount of available space in the exhibit location, will help you determine what types of materials you should use when constructing the exhibit.

Held in the lobby of Old Dominion University's Patricia W. and J. Douglas Perry Library in October 2008, the "School Desegregation in Norfolk, Virginia" exhibit was used to publicize the related online exhibit (http://www.lib.odu.edu/special/schooldesegregation/index.htm) and the archives. The physical exhibit was installed to coincide with city-wide events that commemorated the end of Massive Resistance (state-mandated school segregation) and was used as a backdrop for a press conference by the university president and mayor of Norfolk. *Photograph by Karen Vaughan, courtesy of Old Dominion University Libraries.*

One final factor in creating exhibits is politics, both internal and external. Always consider the reason behind the exhibit and its intent. Keep in mind key players such as board members, possible donors, or members. Before putting anything on display, make sure that it is not controversial, unless that is the intent of the display. If you know that you will be displaying materials that may be offensive or controversial in nature, you should include a disclaimer to remind viewers that you are simply displaying historic materials and that the views reflected in those materials are not the views held by your institution. You also need to keep in mind that although some of your materials may be historical in nature, the creator or his or her family members may still be alive. If you intend to put personal materials on display, check the deed of gift for any restrictions and talk to the donor or his or her family. Make sure your labels are as accurate as possible and that all names are spelled correctly no matter what, because you never know who will come by. If you are uncertain about any text or materials that you intend to display, meet with your boss or governing body to discuss the possible implications.

If you have a display case that requires regular rotation, create displays that you can reuse. One way to do this is to put together panels that can be put up by anyone at any time. If you also plan to use three-dimensional objects, keep a list of what you used and their locations so that you can easily pull them out again the next time you need them. It would also be beneficial to take photos of the display once it is in place so that you can use it as a reference point to recreate the exhibit at a later time. Keep an exhibit folder that includes the list of items in the exhibit, photographs, and any other information or instructions that may be needed to recreate the exhibit.

Sarah Minegar shares documents from the Lloyd W. Smith Archival Collection, at Morristown National Historical Park, with Roxbury High School students. *Photograph courtesy of Joni Rowe.*

Using Archival Materials in the Classroom

Not all archivists will reach out to students, but sometimes going into the classroom or bringing the students to the archives can be beneficial to both parties. If you are a college or university archivist, you may be required to step into the classroom, but many lone arrangers have no obligation to interact with students. If you do find yourself in a position to work with students, here are some ideas to help you show them how engaging archives can be.

High school and college students. A good way to engage students at this age is to "play archives." You can do this in the archives itself or in the classroom. Find out how many students you will have in the class ahead of time and plan to divide them into groups of three or four. Find materials in your collections that would be easy to work with and interesting to the students. Pick one or two boxes from a collection for each group; the more variety among the collections, the better. Create worksheets to accompany the boxes that give a brief overview of the collection and the types of materials they are looking at. For example, you could tell them that the materials in group A are institutional records. Describe the overall collection and what the term *institutional record* means. Each worksheet should have two to four questions about the collection for the students to answer. When you have pulled the boxes and created the worksheets, gather your materials. If you don't want to use originals, you can use photocopies or duplicates. When using originals, ask a colleague or teacher to assist you in monitoring the security of the collections. Bring pencils to class with the worksheets. If necessary, bring white gloves or other materials that might be needed for the students to get hands-on experience.

Once you are in the classroom or the students have arrived in the archives, tell them about the activity and ask them to clear off their desks, put all bags on the floor, and put away all pens, markers, food, and drinks. If you are in the archives, explain the reading room rules, or, if you have a list of rules, hand out the list to the students. They may have questions about why certain rules are in place. Try to make the classroom or the archives a friendly and inviting place.

Once they are settled, ask students if any of them have ever been to the archives. Ask anyone who answers *yes* to describe the archives, why he or she was there, and what the experience was like. If no one has experience with archives, ask students what they think an archive is. Be sure to talk to them about what to expect, should they decide to use an archive for research. Break them into groups and give each group a worksheet and the accompanying boxes. Explain that they need to keep the materials in order and that these are irreplaceable. Allow them at least twenty minutes with the materials and time to fill out their worksheets. Walk around the room and allow them to ask questions about the materials and archives. Depending on how much time you have, let students do a brief presentation about their box of materials. Some good questions to have them answer are "Why would a researcher use these materials?" and "What was the most interesting thing you found?"

Elementary and middle school students. Depending on the types of materials you have in your collection, you may want to use only reproductions or duplicates of materials with these students. They may not be able to fully grasp the concept of archives at this point. Objects or photographs will be better received than photocopies of documents. Look for items that are colorful, intricate, or relevant to a topic they are covering in their schoolwork or something familiar to them. Simple things like the old version of their school logo or photos of a well-known area will draw them in. They will also be attracted to anything that they would find strange, such as a typewriter or other outdated technology.

Depending on the age of the students and the overall purpose of your visit, you may want to do a compare-and-contrast exercise, such as compare a photo of something then with a photo of something now. Another option is a "Where's

Waldo?"-type exercise in which students have a physical object in hand but have to identify it in an old photo.

Working with students can be rewarding and challenging. Expect to get questions that you will not be able to answer, but be prepared to follow up with an answer or point them to resources where they can find the answer themselves. Don't expect students of any age to totally grasp the concept of archives, as this may be their first encounter with archival materials. The idea is to introduce them to a new concept and hope that they have a valuable educational experience.

Oral Histories

Oral history programs can be good for both reference and outreach among your constituents. Organizing and starting an oral history program can seem daunting, but it doesn't have to be. If you want to start an oral history program, frame the program with a focus on your needs and budget.

If you are starting a new oral history program, here are some things to keep in mind:

- How important is this program in relation to your other work?
- Why are you collecting oral histories?
- Do you plan to limit the program by number of interviews or run it for a limited number of months/years?
- What is your budget?
- Where will you conduct these oral histories?
- Who will conduct the interviews?
- Will you need to travel or will the interviewees travel to you?
- How will you organize, maintain, and preserve these histories?
- Do you plan to put them online?
- Will they be transcribed or searchable?

Once you have answered these questions, you can begin to frame the program. Determine the type of equipment you will need to conduct these interviews. Keep in mind where and how you will record these oral histories. You may only need to secure an audio recording device such as a digital recorder. If you plan to conduct video interviews, set up a camera on a tripod or have someone operate the camera, or be prepared to operate the camera and have someone else conduct the interview.

You also need to take into account the legal implications of an oral history program. Make sure that anyone providing you with an oral history understands why you are doing the oral history and what it will be used for. Have them sign an agreement stating that they willfully and knowingly participated in the project. If you plan to put any part of these oral histories on your website, whether they are audio, video, or transcripts, be sure to indicate on the agreement that you intend to make these histories public, not only to visitors who come to your archives but also through the Web. In some cases an interviewee may want to restrict part or the entire interview for a set time period because of information that may be disclosed in the interview. Work with your general counsel's office or ask an outside legal consultant to advise you when drafting these agreements.

Depending on how you structure the program, you may want to disclose your intended questions to the interviewee ahead of time to allow him or her to prepare for the interview. It will be a better interview if you are both prepared ahead of time.[4]

Community Outreach

Most organizations work in some capacity with their local community. Even corporations have various community outreach programs. Although archives aren't always a component of these community outreach programs, they are often involved in communicating the history of the organization. The outreach activities you provide should be a positive experience for both you and the community.

So how do you get the larger community involved? That will depend on your institution's mission and how involved it is with the larger community. Your institution may have already established events for the community, and there may be opportunities to start new programs. First, take a look at any existing programs that happen on a yearly basis. Open houses offer a good opportunity to reach out. This does not mean that you need to throw open the doors to your archives and allow everyone to walk through casually. Open houses take many forms and may be as simple as setting up a table in an area outside of the archives. Consider creating a standard informational poster that you can take with you and set up on a table at open houses, conferences, workshops, and other events where you might find potential users. You can also create simple brochures that talk about your services, fees, hours, website, and so on. It doesn't need to be elaborate, just informational. Other quick informational pieces you can create are bookmarks, flyers, and postcards, all of which you can easily produce in-house.

A gathering of students interested in learning more about archives at the NASA Ames Research Center History Office, Moffett Field, California. *Photograph courtesy of April Gage.*

CHORALLY INVITED! A CASE STUDY IN OUTREACH
BY CHRISTINA PRUCHA

The American Choral Directors Association, based in Oklahoma City, is a professional organization for choral directors with about 18,000 members worldwide. The members are choir directors who direct various types of choirs, from community children's choirs to university and college choirs. The organization has been in Oklahoma City since 2004, yet, many guests comment, "Wow, I never knew this was here." The question then becomes, "How do we make people aware of us and what we offer? How do we become part of the larger community?" As the archivist, I have one of the most visible positions in the organization. The archives is open to all, and I have fielded calls and e-mails from members, choral enthusiasts, and the press. Anyone with a question about choral music has the potential to contact us with his or her request. As the association began to grapple with the question of how to become known to the community, I became the one to tackle the issue.

When your organization exists to promote excellence in choral music, it makes sense that an outreach project would incorporate choirs as much as possible. And, because the goal was to introduce the association to the community, it made even more sense that the first outreach project should bring in local choirs to share their talent, show support for our local choirs, and help build awareness in the community of who we are and what we do.

The project also serves to help our staff remember why we exist as an organization. The staff constantly interacts with choirs and choir directors, but they rarely get to attend choral concerts. Only two of our eleven staff members have choral backgrounds. The short choral sessions expose everyone to different types of choral music and reminds them of what occurs as a result of our work.

We began this outreach effort with support from my executive director in the summer of 2009. We decided to bring in local choirs every month for a brown-bag lunch series. The community has access to a tremendous resource in recordings, choral history, choral performance, and current practice in the choral arts, yet most people in our immediate community do not know about it. This series was an effort to change that. Choirs were invited to our museum space to sing in a 45-minute concert over the lunch hour. It was free and open to the public, who were invited to bring their lunch and enjoy a short concert with us. People who attended became aware of us and what we do. The archives was involved because we had more experience with outreach within our organization.

In fall 2009 we started inviting area choirs to participate and explained the conditions. People would be entering and exiting and eating, and there were no appropriate warm-up spaces. In other words, this was to be a highly relaxed, casual concert. We also offered to pay parking for the groups, as we do not have free parking around our building, and because the choirs were giving up their lunch hour to perform, we offered to provide lunch for them. We were able to line up choirs from September through December 2009.

A few weeks before the first event, we began to advertise. As we had no budget for advertising, we used community calendars and our local conventions and visitors bureau to spread our message throughout the downtown community. We also created flyers that were placed in public places like the library throughout the downtown area. Our total advertising cost was about $25 for the first session.

We were able to save money in other ways by using tables and chairs that we already owned and obtaining secondhand risers from our city's civic center. We were fortunate enough to have our own seven-foot Steinway, although we did need to buy a conductor's stand. This was the extent of our expenditures.

In December we obtained a matching grant from the Oklahoma Arts Council to help fund our outreach program for the month. The grant helped pay for costs associated with the event and helped to reduce our overall costs.

We have had mixed success with this program so far, and we've had some challenges. Our building is located two blocks west of the tunnel that connects most of the downtown area. When the weather turns bad and the winds pick up, no one wants to come outside and walk to our building. So, while we had a very nice attendance of twenty people for our first installment in September, our attendance in December was only one-quarter of that.

Other than the weather, we have encountered only minor problems. In November we were unable to find a choir to perform. Schools do not easily release students from classes and most choirs are very busy performing for their holiday programs. Therefore, we had to cancel and make up for it by holding two sessions in December.

The outreach effort has helped people understand who we are and why we exist. The community learned about our history and that we hold a collection that represents choral music over the last fifty years. They know where to come and where to send people who have questions about choral music. Overall it has been a success, but we still have a way to go in building a following—however, creating a following is what counts.

As lone arrangers, some of us serve in colleges, others serve churches, and still other serve in corporations of all types. Given the variety of archives and the often small budgets and staffs we have to work with, I urge lone arrangers to think about what their organization excels at and to build an outreach program around that to draw in potential users, create awareness, and give back to the community. As lone arrangers, we do not have to perform outreach alone. Draw in field experts, celebrate your organization's strengths, and think outside the box. If a lone arranger in a choral music archive can do that, so can you.

When working on an outreach project, think of creative ways to engage your potential audience. Some things to keep in mind are:

- Why would someone use the archives?

- What are some of the most interesting/potentially useful items or collections?

- How do the archival collections connect to the larger community?

- How can you engage the community in a hands-on way?

Besides creating flyers and brochures, think of other ways to actively engage your community. Perhaps you can create a history day with re-creations of games, plays, or other activities that are no longer done. The more actively

Open House at Indiana University South Bend. The Open House was tied in with the Campus Theme, "The Meaning of Work," by displaying items from the Labor Collections. Included in the display was a table with the request "Please Help Us ID These Photos." As part of the Open House there were also archives-related giveaways. *Photograph courtesy of Alison Stankrauff.*

engaged people are, the more interested they will be in your organization and, hopefully, the archives at large.

Using Social Media

For those of us just starting to look at the possibilities that the Web can provide, what exactly is social media? Social media takes us beyond the traditional website and includes such things as blogs, podcasting, wikis, Twitter, Facebook, Flickr, YouTube, Mashups, and Widgets. These new tools allow us to reach out to our existing constituents and beyond. Archivists have adapted these applications to do everything from promoting specific events to providing a continuous narrative to its followers. So how can lone arrangers take advantage of this trend?

Before using social media, weigh the pros and cons for your institution and determine what applications will work best for you. Consider the following questions:

- What is your mission and how can social media advance that mission?

- How much time do you have to put into maintaining and updating content?

- What kind of content do you want to put out on the Web?

- How do you want to present that content?

- Can you feed content to social media applications already started by your parent organization?

- What kind of content can you legally use/display?

When considering how much time you want to spend on maintaining and updating social media applications, think about setting a schedule for yourself and look at ways to load content in advance and have it released on the dates and times that you preset. If you can, work with your organization by providing content to the person that is in charge of maintaining your institution's social media applications. Try not to compete with your own organization and coordinate your efforts.

One way to capture the attention of constituents and beyond is to attach images to interesting facts. Consider using multiple applications by adding links so that users are drawn to additional content. For example, if you use Twitter, you can add a link to an image in Flickr, a video on YouTube, or a podcast. Social media is a good way to attract new and younger constituents as well as longtime patrons. It will help your patrons and potential patrons find out about your offerings, events, and other information.

Just as with exhibits, when using social media tools, you need to consider the political implications within your institution as well as copyright laws. If you are uploading photographs or other information on the Web, make sure that you have the rights to do so. The Web is even more public than an exhibit case at your institution, and it is much more visible. Before using social media, talk to possible stakeholders, review deeds of gift (if you have them), and think about what kinds of content you can and should share with the world.

Conclusion

Reference and outreach activities are essential to the success of any archival program. Whether your constituents are internal or external, the reason you exist is to provide a service to them. Create and maintain tools to make your work easier. The more organized you are, the less time and effort you will spend the next time around.

When starting an internal advocacy or outreach program, be creative and use your existing resources to help you achieve your goals. Work on ways to engage both existing users and potential users through physical or online exhibits as well as social media. Whether in the classroom or in a display case, your efforts will go a long way to promoting good will and a positive long-term relationship between you and your constituents.

NOTES

[1] Richard Pearce-Moses, *A Glossary of Archival and Records Terminology* (Chicago: Society of American Archivists, 2005), available at http://www.archivists.org/glossary/index.asp.

[2] For more information on the ethics behind access to archival materials, see the ALA–SAA Joint Statement on Access to Original Materials in Libraries, Archives, and Manuscript Repositories available at http://www.archivists.org/statements/alasaa.asp.

[3] For more information on records management, see Chapter 4.

[4] For more information on conducting oral histories, contact the Oral History Association or visit http://www.oralhistory.org.

CHAPTER 7

"How Am I Going to Pay for This?"
Budgeting and Financing Your Archives

In your work in a small shop, budgeting, fundraising, and development probably fall toward the bottom of your priority list. However, the amount of money you have and how much you can bring in will determine the sustainability of your archives. Maintaining an archives is not a money-making enterprise, and your institution will most likely view it as not profitable. It is your job as the archivist to convey the importance of your institution's archives and find ways to make it financially viable to your organization. Through proper budgeting, fundraising, and development activities such as grant writing, you can make your archives a sustainable entity within your organization.

Creating and Setting Up Your Budget

Budgeting can be a new and difficult challenge for lone arrangers. In some cases you may not have a clear-cut budget. If you *are* given a budget, it is usually up to you to determine the line items. If you have a preexisting budget, make sure that the line items match your current needs and adjust them as needed.

Review your budget each year and adjust it as your priorities and funding change. Sometimes funds may be allocated on a case-by-case basis determined by the current cash flow of the organization. This is far from ideal, but it may be out of your control. Even if the organization doesn't officially recognize it, you should have a budget for your own reference to track spending so that you can show your boss what, where, and how you are spending the money. To keep your operations running smoothly, work with your organization to set up a budget that works for both of you.

Here are some essential items to consider including in your budget:

- Supplies—both archival supplies and basic office supplies
- Office equipment purchasing/maintenance/replacement
- Shelving and storage cabinets
- Computer and software needs, including scanners and other hardware

KEY TERMS }

A **line item** in a budget is a breakdown of expenditures that are grouped by departments or costs. You most likely have a lump sum allotted from a larger budget for your archives. Within that lump sum you will have specific "lines" to which the money is allocated. For example, you may have a portion of your budget, or one line item, dedicated to archival supplies.

- Professional development (i.e., workshops, conferences, classes)

- Playback equipment for audiovisual collections—purchasing/ maintenance

- Preservation activities, such as conservation or tools needed for proper storage and housing of materials

- Exhibition expenses—costs associated with printing, mounting, and displaying items

- Records management expenses—off-site storage, shredding, etc.

- Temporary or part-time help expenses

Depending on the scope of your work, you may need to revise your list of included items to cover any other budgeting needs you have. You can also add extra money to your budget with wish-list items so that if you need to cut items from your budget you know what can easily go.

Budgeting is often a touchy subject, particularly when an institution has a small budget or is facing a decline or stagnation in its overall budget. Compromise is the best solution in these cases. As the archivist, you know what your needs are and where you can cut or reduce if necessary. Make your supervisor aware of any significant impacts that could occur in the event of a budget cut. Before meeting to discuss budget matters, put together a list of your needs, how much you think they will cost (be sure to research any figures and have proof of these figures), and what impact there might be if a particular activity or line item is not funded. Beware of "unfunded mandates" that might fall in your lap. These are special projects or major initiatives that your institution may tell you need to be done but give you no funding or extra help to do them. Avoiding those projects is usually not an option; however, be vocal about the impact to your work and other projects that are currently in progress. If funding is crucial to completing a project, make the case that it needs to be added to your budget. Often unfunded mandates go unfulfilled or another project is abandoned while a new, unfunded initiative is fulfilled.

When looking at your budget, consider the possibility of getting outside funding. If your institution already holds an annual fundraiser, such as a "phone-a-thon," or is funded by grants, include those in your budget. Even if you don't currently do any fundraising activities but are planning them for the future, look at budget items that might be funded by those activities. Include any grants that you may apply for and/or receive. Because grants and fundraising are not guaranteed sources of funding, do not count on using that funding to finance any essential operations.

Fundraising

There is no doubt that fundraising is not only an important function for both you and your institution but it is also necessary to sustain an archival program. Fundraising can be as simple as your run-of-the-mill used book sale to a much more elaborate silent auction or gala. The type of fundraising that you and your institution undertake will depend on the resources and time available to carry out any fundraising activity as well as how your organization is structured.

Planning is an important first step in any fundraising initiative. When considering any fundraising activities, keep the following in mind:

- How much will it cost to hold the fundraiser, both in terms of money and time?

- Who will be involved?

- How much money do you anticipate earning?

- What kind of fundraiser is most appropriate for your institution?

- Where will the event take place?

- What is the best date/time for your fundraiser to attract the largest number of people?

- What other ways can you raise funds?

  o A "donate now" button on your website

  o Mailings—e-mail or paper

  o Add the archives to other fundraising activities undertaken by the organization

Once you consider all of these factors, you should be able to put together a fundraiser that will suit your needs.

If your institution has a development office, work on building a strong relationship with the staff there. Building relationships with your supervisor and your development office will help you to build a stronger archival program. Likewise, if your archives is part of a library, you will need to involve the director in any fundraising activities. Your library may also have a friends group; take advantage of their willingness to organize and run fundraisers.

Fundraising should also be a factor in your outreach activities. If you work with other offices or departments in your institution, talk to them about how you can use the archives to both help them and to raise money for the archives. Perhaps you can use an image or images from the archives to create promotional items. Maybe you can find a way to raise money through exhibits. Make it clear that by supporting the archives and its financial stability, they will guarantee that the archives will be able to assist them in the future.

Another issue to consider is charging fees for services. This can be a sensitive subject in some institutions. You may not be allowed to charge fees, but there may be cases where fees are justified. It is fairly common to have a fee schedule in place for services such as photocopying, scanning, printing, and

Planning is an important first step in any fundraising initiative.

any other reproduction services that involve the use of supplies. You may also be required to charge for permission fees to cover any copyrights involved in the reproduction of an item. It is less common to charge for research services or to charge an admission fee, but it may be a factor to consider, depending on your institution and funding situation. These fees are often nominal and will not provide you with a wealth of income, but they should cover the cost of supplies needed to process a request or cover the cost of your time.

Finally, fundraising opportunities may happen during the acquisition of a new collection. If someone donates a large collection, consider asking them for a monetary gift to accompany the collection. The best way to do this is to explain to the donor that the gift will take time to process and will require money to cover the cost of time and supplies needed to properly arrange and describe the collection. Some donors may not be amenable to this suggestion; however, if you give the donor examples of time, money, and potential usage, they may be more inclined to give you some funds for the project. You should ask for money, particularly if the donor specifies that the collection be processed and accessible within a certain timeframe.

Grant Writing

Due to time constraints, grant writing is one of the most difficult tasks for a lone arranger. You are already buried in work, and writing grants can be daunting. Finding and applying for grants is time-consuming and not always a guarantee of funding. Depending on the grant, it could mean taking on a new initiative. Large grants from the federal government, such as the National Endowment for the Humanities (NEH) and the National Historical Publications and Records Commission (NHPRC), are easy to identify and would fund many of your day-to-day activities; however, applying for these grants can take a lot of time, while requiring standards and matching funds that may not be available to you. An alternative to these larger granting agencies is a number of smaller granting organizations. Sometimes it is difficult to find these organizations and to come up with a project that fits the scope of their grants. All of this may seem impossible for a small institution, but it doesn't have to be.

Before you start looking for grants, investigate whether the institution has applied for a grant in the past, what the grant was, and whether or not the application was successful. If you have a development office, talk to the appropriate person in that office about the possibility of applying for a grant. You will most likely need to educate development staff as well as any other non-archivists or librarians about why you want a grant and how it can be helpful to your work. When talking to your development office, discuss what needs to be in place to apply for a grant, such as proper tax reporting and fund distribution. Does your institution already have a system in place for filing electronic grant applications? Where will the money go and how will it be disbursed? You will need to have several conversations with your superiors and/or development office throughout the process.

Start by looking for local foundations and smaller granting organizations rather than large government grants. You can find smaller local organizations through The Foundation Center.[1] If you are located in a large metropolitan area, you may have access to one of their libraries to research granting organizations and even take some free or low-cost grant writing workshops. If you do not live in an area where you can physically go to their library or attend workshops, The Foundation Center offers free online courses and resources to help you get started. The Foundation Center also offers databases and other publications that can assist you in finding and writing grants. If you do not have the money to purchase these publications, check your local library to see if they are available there. Another option is to look for other local organizations that offer grant writing classes.[2] Research your options thoroughly. It is best to start with a smaller, less complicated grant process before moving on to larger grants. If you can prove that you have had success with a smaller grant, it will be easier to obtain a larger one later.

If you are considering applying for a grant, the first step is to identify your need(s):

- Why do you need a grant?

- Is it for a special project, or are you looking for additional money for a capital campaign or renovation project?

- What kind of project is it (preservation, processing)?

- Will the project require additional staff, equipment, and supplies?

- Can you fulfill the requirements of the grant?

- Will it help you sustain your archives? How?

Answering these questions and identifying your needs will help you focus your efforts. You should have a well-thought-out plan before spending the time and effort to research and write a grant.

Once you have established what you need to support the grant, it is time to look for opportunities. Start with examples of both successful and unsuccessful grant applications. It is helpful to look at the types of grants that smaller institutions received to get a better idea of the scale of the project and the amount of funding that was given. Talk to other archivists in small shops who may have received a grant, and find out what type of grant they obtained, for how much, and for what type of project.

If you can't find smaller grant opportunities that match your needs, or you would rather apply for a grant from a larger government granting organization such as the National Endowment for the Humanities (NEH), the National Historical Publications and Records Commission (NHPRC), the Institute for Museum and Library Services (IMLS), or Council on Libraries and Information Resources (CLIR), you may want to start with something like the

NEH Preservation Assistance Grant for Small Institutions. This grant will give you a few thousand dollars to get some basic preservation supplies such as a data logger, shelving, or assistance writing disaster or preservation plans.

When you have identified the grant that best suits your needs, be sure to read all the fine print to make certain that you submit the application properly. It is easy to forget something and, therefore, easy to lose a grant opportunity in the process. Another important part of grant writing is your budget. Different grants require different types of budgets. Most grants require matching funds, which means the institution must be willing to supply or pay for approximately half of the project budget. These matching funds may include the cost of your salary, your benefits, the purchase or maintenance of a database, equipment, and facilities. This may also mean that your institution will need to purchase equipment, pay half of the salary of an additional archivist for the project, or other costs. Before applying for a grant, be sure that your institution is willing to take on the match for the project.

Although grant writing can be difficult, there is help available. If you are working on a preservation assistance grant, you can contact any number of regional nonprofit conservation organizations. Sometimes the granting agency will also provide you with assistance and even require that you submit a draft before submitting your final grant application. Grant writing workshops are offered all over the country and can provide you with additional resources and assistance for grants.

When writing your grant application, keep in mind that you need to fulfill any promises you make. If the grant requires that you upload records to WorldCat or put up finding aids in EAD, you must be capable of carrying out your obligations. You must set yourself up to do this even before you submit the grant application. Make sure that you have the space and equipment to fulfill all of the grant requirements as well as the ability to train any additional staff required for the project.

Depending on the complexity of the grant, you may need to set up deadlines and an overall time line to complete the grant application to be sure that you submit it on time. It is helpful to block out several hours at a time when you can work uninterrupted. Also, build in time to have others review your work for content and grammatical errors.

Once you have submitted a grant application, your job is not done. It may take a few weeks to a few months to get an answer, so take the time to prepare yourself and your institution as if you are going to receive the money. This does not mean you need to start ordering equipment and posting job descriptions; however, it does mean that you should identify what to purchase and prepare your workspace. If you do receive the money, you can hit the ground running. If you do not receive the grant, you can usually request copies of the reviewers' comments. These will help you identify why you did not get the grant and what you might change if you intend to apply again.

Finally, if you do receive a grant, you must be able to manage it properly. Allot sufficient time to manage the grant budget and any additional staff or workflow demands, as well as preparation of periodic reports that the granting agency may request. Some grants only require a final report while others require regular reports be submitted throughout the life of the grant. Be sure to carefully review any reporting guidelines before submitting reports. Depending on the length of the grant, you will need to make sure that you can accommodate the extra workload over that time period. Do not take on any new or extensive projects if you have applied for a grant. The funding agency will judge your institution not only on its creativity but also on the ability to carry out the grant successfully.

Development

Most nonprofit institutions have a development staff who work to fund the activities of that institution. This department can work with you to identify potential donors, funding sources, and granting organizations. A good solid working relationship with your development staff can mean stable financial ground for the archives. Even if you don't have a development office, you can become the development person for the archives.

Working with your development office should go hand-in-hand with your outreach activities for the archives. Not only should the development staff know what you are doing and how you are making a difference, but potential donors also need to know this information. If you are not communicating your importance to both the institution and the community it serves, it will be difficult to raise the capital needed to continue operations. It is also important that you make the development office aware of what you can do for them.

When you are talking about the archives to your development office or your constituents, you need to be able to answer the following questions:

- What is the purpose of the archives?
- How does it benefit the organization?
- Whom does it serve?
- What are the archives' needs?
- If someone were to donate money, how would it be spent?

Outline clear goals and objectives for your fundraising efforts. Anyone trying to raise money for the archives needs to know why they should help you when they have other issues and concerns. Make the archives a priority for them.

If you do not have a development office and you are part of a larger department within an organization, such as a library or historical society, consider starting a development committee or work with committees you may already have in place. This committee might also function as your marketing committee.

KEY TERMS }

Development means the expansion of financial resources as well as relationships with outside people, companies, and organizations for the betterment of the organization. A development office works with people and other organizations to secure additional financing and partnerships to accomplish common goals.

Explore ways to reach out to prospective donors and constituents to involve them in your organization as well as ways to engage them in fundraising activities.

Whether your development staff consists of one or ten people, their knowledge of donor relations, grant writing, and fundraising will provide you with the support you require to raise the money needed to continue your operations. If you don't have a development office, you should learn the skills needed to raise the profile of your archives and work with potential donors to secure your financial future. Organizations like The Foundation Center offer free courses in-person and online to help you learn more about development activities.

Donor Relations

One important aspect of working as a lone arranger is that you become the face of your institution's archives. It is a fact that the majority of money donated to nonprofits comes from private donors, not from grants or corporate gifts. Whether you are fulfilling a routine reference request or specifically talking to someone about financial matters, you are the one that needs to make that person feel good about your archives and the services it provides. Donor relations can make or break your institution. If you can't be bothered with them, they won't be bothered with you.

In the course of your daily work, you will come across people ranging from coworkers to researchers. You need to be the messenger for the archives and spread the word about all of the hard work you are doing and how it benefits those around you. One researcher may be so grateful for the information you provided for his or her research that that researcher will send money to support your operations. The ten-year-old report that you found for your president may have saved him or her some work, resulting in an increase in your budget. You never know who may take up your cause or make a donation to the archives. If people feel good about the work you do and have a good relationship with you, the monetary benefits will follow.

Many archivists seem to think that because they haven't received money in the past, they shouldn't expect to receive money now. This negative attitude only weakens your financial stability and your overall message. The main reason people give money is because they have been asked to donate. Perhaps in the past no one bothered to ask. You can change this culture by asking potential donors to fund projects or provide money to your general operating budget. Do not be afraid to hear *no*. That initial *no* may become a *yes* in the future if that person can see your hard work come to fruition.

Annual reports are also important in improving donor relations. Many nonprofit institutions create an annual report as part of their regular operations. If the archives is not represented in that report, see if you can include information such as new acquisitions, monetary donations, reference

MANAGING A GRANT PROJECT WITH MINIMAL STAFF

BY BARBARA AUSTEN

The Connecticut Historical Society (CHS) was founded in 1825 by interested, civic-conscious, well-to-do men from Hartford, Connecticut. Initially a library, the institution accepted more and more objects (or curiosities) as time went on. The early establishment of the Society meant that it was able to collect many founding documents of Connecticut and the United States (which, in 1825, was recent history).

The cataloging of books, manuscripts, and objects was haphazard at best and certainly not up to the standards we have developed and come to expect today. The museum cataloging was upgraded starting in the 1970s and today is done using The Museum System. Library materials were first cataloged by hand, then on typed cards in a card catalog. The Society's staff began cataloging printed and manuscript materials and adding them to OCLC in 1984 and later into our own online catalog (Voyager). It was obvious that a lot of collections did not have a record in the online catalog, as there had been no retrospective conversion for the manuscripts.

When I arrived at the CHS in 2004, my first task was to inventory the manuscript collections before moving them for the renovation of the storage area. The next task was to increase access to the manuscripts.

The data collected for the inventory and put into a Microsoft Access database was supplemented by examining the accession logs beginning in 1839, as well as records in the online and card catalogs. The information gathered included the accession number of the collection or item, creator, title, location, presence or absence of any catalog record, the amount of processing done, and notes on extent and hints as to locations ("filed with Talcott Papers"). Analysis of the data indicated that thousands of collections and individual items were neither included in the card catalog nor the online version. The concatenation of our revised institutional focus on access, the introduction of "More Product/Less Process" (MPLP), and the change in NHPRC grant priorities to provide funding for cataloging backlogs led to CHS submitting an application for and receiving a two-year grant to reduce the backlog by 900 records, or about 600 linear feet. The project started in September 2008.

With the inventory as a guide, I selected the top priorities for cataloging, using the criteria of size (we targeted the largest), the oldest material, and research potential (namely, founding "fathers" and political figures). As a secondary collection, I decided to focus on the extensive holdings of account books. In the second year of the grant, we added genealogical research collections as a tertiary focus.

The Society, as stated, already had a subscription to OCLC. The work flow could easily be applied to the backlog project—examine the collections, create MARC records with Connexion Client, upload the records to OCLC, and then download them into the institution's OPAC. As a result, the Society did not consider using a different cataloging or management system.

To address a total of 900 records, the decision was made to institute MPLP. In fact, the approach was essentially required by NHPRC. That meant the project archivist and I would not fully process any collections. However, we would keep track of those collections that needed fuller processing to collect data for a future grant proposal. A procedure manual that I prepared outlined the differences between minimal, adequate, and full processing, noting that minimal was all that was required for this project. I developed CHS cataloging guidelines, including the MARC fields to be used (we created minimal records) and suggested subject headings.

It took two months to hire a project archivist with the right combination of archival background and experience with using Connexion Client for cataloging. The successful candidate started September 1, 2008, and immediately began cataloging account books. This enabled her to gain a sense of the documentation for the collections and become comfortable with the cataloging guidelines.

Within Connexion Client, I created a single file for all grant-funded cataloging. That way we could chart our progress and keep the project work separate from daily cataloging. I reviewed all catalog records before they were uploaded to OCLC and then into our online catalog.

Implementing MPLP proved a challenge. It was very difficult not to impose any order on a totally disorganized collection or not to put materials into acid-free folders. We found that we had to adjust our application of MPLP for each collection. Those that had particularly old and/or fragile materials generally received more processing, sorting items at least by year and putting the paper in acid-free folders. With more modern collections, we simply put items into folders if they were not already in one, created a box list, and then cataloged the collection.

As we proceeded, we updated the inventory to indicate that a catalog record had been created. We also noted the need for additional processing, the need for conservation, the presence of photographs and newspaper clippings (which we did not photocopy), the presence of documents with high monetary value (autographs), and items that could be scanned and added to Connecticut History Online, a cooperative digital library.

It took some time, but we also got into a routine of checking the museum catalog for related objects and then adding that information to the MARC record and the museum catalog. I have used interns and volunteers for fuller processing, and they create finding aids or at least a brief scope and content note so we can create catalog records.

Setting priorities in the abstract was not always practical. Our goal was to process the largest collections first, mainly because most of them had never had any access. However, we found some small collections more historically valuable than larger ones, such as the papers of John Cotton Smith (twenty-third governor of Connecticut). After the top-priority collections were cataloged, it was hard to decide how to proceed. In the inventory, I created a query to find only those collections she had marked for the grant project before the start of the project. That list included much more than the initial 900. Once that numerical goal was reached, we simply went through the list item by item to reduce the overall backlog.

One unstated goal for the project was to create collection files as each collection or item was cataloged— accession records, deeds of gift, and so on. It became much too easy to focus on cataloging to reach the numerical goal and not on gathering documentation, or checking the inventory for duplicate records, or checking authorities both on OCLC and our own catalog. Essentially, I needed to provide more supervision at the beginning of the project to establish best practices.

However, with a staff of only two, and with one (being myself) devoting only part of her time to the project, we met our stated goal by the end of the first year. Everything after that was gravy! We proved MPLP can be used with older manuscript collections and that 900 records in two years is not an impossible goal.

statistics, and any outreach efforts that you did throughout the year. Donors want to see how their money is being used, and when non-donors see what you can do they may be inspired to contribute money the following year.

If you are working with potential donors, whether they intend to give money or collections, bear in mind that you need to turn on the charm and become genuinely interested in what they have to say. Talk to them about what you can do for them and how their donations will make a difference to not only your organization but to your researchers. Refine your people skills as well as your message. This will promote good will among your constituents and give them confidence in donating their money or collections. This is also referred to as *cultivating* donors, meaning that you may need to develop a relationship with a donor over time so that he or she becomes acquainted with your archives and its operations before they feel comfortable donating a large amount of money.

Conclusion

Budgeting, fundraising, grant writing, and development can become a low priority. These are activities that you may perceive to be out of your hands; however, you should never forget them. The only way to sustain the archives—and your job security—is to work to secure your financial future; therefore, being concerned with finances is a critical part of your work. Do not look at these issues as separate from your archival mission.

Keeping track of your budget is crucial to planning for projects and fundraising activities. Knowing what your available resources are can help you to identify areas where you need to increase funding. Tracking your spending allows you to spend your money wisely and get the most from every dollar.

Remember, you are the public face of your archives. Keeping both internal and external patrons happy should be at the top of your to-do list. Money often comes when it is least expected from those whom you would least expect to give. You can enhance donor relationships by working with your development office. Finally, look for ways to incorporate fundraising and grant writing into your daily workflow. Not only can these be a learning experience, they can be fun too!

NOTES

[1] See http://foundationcenter.org.

[2] For more information about finding grants and grant writing workshops, see Appendix B of this book.

Conclusion

As a lone arranger, you face major challenges every day with limited budgets and little to no staffing. Despite these challenges, you are able to accomplish multiple tasks in a single day—from managing yourself to managing your budget. Although your daily tasks may be overwhelming at times, you have the power to influence how your archives are run, what materials you will collect, what you will discard, and how the collections will be organized. As you continue your work as a lone arranger, keep these recommendations in mind:

- Keep yourself organized and do not try to take on too many projects at once.

- Know your limits and make yourself heard.

- Concentrate on tasks that will make your life easier.

- Foster good relationships with the people inside your organization.

- Network with other lone arrangers and archivists.

- Treat your patrons and donors with respect, as they may become your best source for funding and support.

- Use all available resources to get the job done, including things that are free or have a low cost.

- Be a strong advocate for the archives; without you there would be no archives.

Working in a small shop may be challenging, but these tips will help you through some of the daily obstacles of being a lone arranger.

Connecting with your peers—both archivists and fellow lone arrangers—is essential to your professional growth and your ability to adapt and change to meet the needs of your constituents. Collaborate with other lone arrangers in similar situations by joining listservs, social networks, and local or regional associations. Although you may work by yourself in your physical place, you can connect with hundreds of lone arrangers both near and far to share ideas and help each other in times of need. Working with other archivists toward similar goals can keep you from feeling isolated and make you feel confident in the work that you are doing. These professional contacts will prove to be one of your greatest resources.

Whether you are the first archivist of your archives or the tenth, working as a lone arranger in that setting is no easy feat. You need to review what previous archivists have done and either start from scratch or improve the existing situation. When working alone, it is important to keep in mind that although

Connecting with your peers—both archivists and fellow lone arrangers—is essential to your professional growth and your ability to adapt and change to meet the needs of your constituents.

you should do your best, you should not get hung up on perfection. It is easy for those who have been formally trained as archivists to focus too much on how something "should" be done while losing sight of what really needs to be done. Look at archival standards as a goal to aim for but don't feel as though you have failed if you do not meet those goals. When it comes to managing collections, any structure is better than no structure.

It is easy to become overwhelmed by all of the work that may come your way, but it is essential to take things in stride and learn to say no, while still trying your best to meet the demands of your job. At times, you may need to keep several activities going simultaneously to carry out your full range of responsibilities. If you are organized from the beginning, you will have to spend less time and effort carrying out your responsibilities in the future.

Your constituents, whether internal or external, are the reason you exist. It is important to work on ways to engage both existing users and potential users through physical or online exhibits, finding aids, classes, Web pages, or social media. Whether in the classroom or in a display case, your efforts can go a long way to promote good will and foster a positive long-term relationship between you and your constituents. Remember, you are the public face of your archives, so keeping both internal and external patrons happy should be at the top of your to-do list. In the end it is our work that shapes the history of our organization and informs our community.

As a lone arranger, you must carefully balance your responsibilities to the organization and your patrons with limited resources, but remember that you are not alone. There is a wealth of resources available to guide you through your daily tasks. By tapping into those resources, you can achieve greater levels of success by making your archives invaluable to its institution or community.

APPENDIX A

Selected Readings

The sources in this selected bibliography provide additional information on the specific topics covered in each chapter. Some works are listed for more than one chapter because they cover a range of topics discussed in this book. Most of the works in this bibliography were published in the last ten years and account for changes in technology and the way archivists work. However, some titles published before 2000 are included because they are the only publications of their kind on a particular topic. Many of these titles can be found in the Society of American Archivists bookstore or may be available through your local library. Some titles may only be available by purchasing them through other venues, such as an out-of-print bookseller.

Chapter 1

Carmichael, David W. *Organizing Archival Records: A Practical Method of Arrangement & Description for Small Archives.* Walnut Creek, CA: AltaMira Press, 2004.

Dearstyne, Bruce W. *Leading and Managing Archives and Records Programs: Strategies for Success.* New York: Neal-Schuman Publishers, 2008.

Hunter, Gregory S. *Developing and Maintaining Practical Archives*, 2nd ed. New York: Neal-Schuman Publishers, 2003.

Kurtz, Michael J. *Managing Archival & Manuscript Repositories.* Chicago: Society of American Archivists, 2004.

McFarland, Colleen. "Rethinking the Business of Small Archives." *Archival Issues* 31, no. 2 (2007): 137–149.

McFarland, Colleen, and Courtney Yevich. "The Business of Archives: Managing Time, People, and Collections in the 21st Century." *Archival Outlook* (September/October 2009): 6, 33.

O'Toole, James M., and Richard Cox. *Understanding Archives and Manuscripts.* Chicago: Society of American Archivists, 2006.

Pearce-Moses, Richard. *A Glossary of Archival and Records Terminology.* Chicago: Society of American Archivists, 2005. Also available at http://www.archivists.org/glossary/index.asp.

Pevar, Susan. "Success as a Lone Arranger: Setting Priorities and Getting the Job Done." *Journal of Archival Organization* 3, no. 1 (2005): 51–60.

Phillips, Faye. "Developing Collecting Policies for Manuscript Collections." *American Archivist* 47 (Winter 1984): 39–41.

Pugh, Mary Jo. *Providing Reference Services for Archives and Manuscripts.* Archival Fundamentals Series II. Chicago: Society of American Archivists, 2005.

Stankrauff, Alison. "On Being a Lone Arranger." *Indiana Libraries* 27, no. 3 (2008): 21–23.

Wythe, Deborah, ed. *Museum Archives: An Introduction*, 2nd ed. Chicago: Society of American Archivists, 2004.

Yakel, Elizabeth. *Starting an Archives.* Chicago: Society of American Archivists; Metuchen, NJ: Scarecrow Press, 1994.

Chapter 2

Boles, Frank. *Selecting and Appraising Archives and Manuscripts.* Chicago: Society of American Archivists, 2005.

Carmicheal, David W. *Organizing Archival Records: A Practical Method of Arrangement and Description for Small Archives.* Walnut Creek, CA: AltaMira Press, 2004.

Craig, Barbara. *Archival Appraisal: Theory and Practice.* Munchen: K. G. Saur, 2004.

Fleckner, John A. *Archives and Manuscripts: Surveys.* Chicago: Society of American Archivists, 1977.

Greene, Mark A., and Dennis Meissner. "More Product, Less Process: Revamping Traditional Archival Processing." *American Archivist* 68 (Fall/ Winter 2005): 208–263.

Ham, F. Gerald. *Selecting and Appraising Archives and Manuscripts.* Chicago: Society of American Archivists, 1993.

Laver, Tara Z. "Do a Good Deed: Deeds of Gift for Manuscript Collections." *Louisiana Libraries* 68, no. 2 (2005): 23–30.

Procter, Margaret, and Michael Cook. *Manual of Archival Description.* Burlington, VT: Gower Publishing, 2000.

Ramos, Marisol, and Alma C. Ortega. *Building a Successful Archival Programme.* Oxford: Chandos Publishing, 2006.

Roe, Kathleen D. *Arranging and Describing Archives and Manuscripts.* Chicago: Society of American Archivists, 2005.

Sample Forms for Archival & Records Management Programs. Chicago: Society of American Archivists and ARMA International, 2002.

Yakel, Elizabeth. *Starting an Archives.* Chicago: Society of American Archivists; Metuchen, NJ: Scarecrow Press, 1994.

Chapter 3

Buelow, Anna E., and Jess Ahmon. *Preparing Collections for Digitization.* London: Facet Publishing, 2010.

Combs, Michele, Mark A. Matienzo, Merrilee Proffitt, and Lisa Spiro. "Over, Under, Around, and Through: Getting Around Barriers to EAD Implementation." OCLC Research, 2010. http://www.oclc.org/research/publications/library/2010/2010-04.pdf.

Dow, Elizabeth H. *Creating EAD-Compatible Finding Guides on Paper.* Lanham, MD: Scarecrow Press, 2005.

———. *Electronic Records in the Manuscript Repository.* Lanham, MD: Scarecrow Press, 2009.

Duhon, Bryant. "Enterprise Content Management: What Is It? Why Should You Care?" *AIIM E-Doc Magazine* 17, no. 6 (November/December 2003).

Hirtle, Peter B., Emily Hudson, and Andrew T. Kenyon. *Copyright & Cultural Institutions: Guidelines for Digitization for U.S. Libraries, Archives, & Museums.* Ithaca, NY: Cornell University Library, 2009. Also available at http://ecommons.cornell.edu.

Lake, David, et al. "Market Survey of Commercially Available Off-the-Shelf Archival Management Software." ICA Study 12. January 2003. http://www.ica.org/en/node/30064.

Spiro, Lisa. *Archival Content Management Systems.* (CD-ROM). Chicago: Society of American Archivists, 2009.

———. "Archival Management Software: A Report for the Council on Library and Information Resources." January 2009. http://www.clir.org/pubs/reports/spiro2009.html.

Swan, Alma. *Open Access Institutional Repositories: A Briefing Paper.* http://www.openscholarship.org/upload/docs/application/pdf/2009-01/open_access_institutional _repositories.pdf.

Westbrook, Bradley D., et al. "The Archivists' Toolkit: Another Step Toward Streamlined Archival Processing." *Journal of Archival Organization* 4, no. 1/2 (2006): 229–253.

Yaco, Sonia. "It's Complicated: Barriers to EAD Implementation." *American Archivist* 71 (Fall/Winter 2008): 456–457.

Chapter 4

Banks, Paul N., and Roberta Pilette. *Preservation Issues and Planning.* Chicago: American Libraries Association, 2000.

Bastian, Jeannette A., and Donna Webber. *Archival Internships: A Guide for Faculty, Supervisors, and Students.* Chicago: Society of American Archivists, 2008.

Dearstyne, Bruce. ed. *Leading and Managing Archives and Records Programs.* New York: Neal-Schuman Publishers, 2008.

Forde, Helen. *Preserving Archives.* London: Facet Publishing, 2007.

Gorman, G. E., and Sydney J. Shep, eds. *Preservation Management for Libraries, Archives and Museums.* London: Facet Publishing, 2006.

Gracy, Karen F. *Film Preservation: Competing Definitions of Value Use, and Practice.* Chicago: Society of American Archivists, 2007.

Kurtz, Michael. *Managing Archival and Manuscript Repositories.* Chicago: Society of American Archivists, 2004.

Prom, Christopher J., and Ellen D. Swain, eds. *College and University Archives: Readings in Theory and Practice.* Chicago: Society of American Archivists, 2008.

Ritzenthaler, Mary Lynn. *Preserving Archives and Manuscripts,* 2nd ed. Chicago: Society of American Archivists, 2010.

Ritzenthaler, Mary Lynn, and Diane Vogt-O'Connor. *Photographs: Archival Care and Management.* Chicago: Society of American Archivists, 2008.

Sample Forms for Archival & Records Management Programs. Chicago: Society of American Archivists and ARMA International, 2002.

Skupsky, Donald J. *Recordkeeping Requirements.* Denver, CO: Information Requirements Clearinghouse, 1994.

———. *Records Retention Procedures: Your Guide to Determine How Long to Keep Your Records and How to Safely Destroy Them!* Denver, CO: Information Requirements Clearinghouse, 1994.

Weeks, Kent M., and Patricia Kussmann. *Record Retention and Disposal: A Manual for College Decision Makers.* Nashville, TN: College Legal Information, 2008.

Yakel, Elizabeth. *Starting an Archives.* Chicago: Society of American Archivists; Metuchen, NJ: Scarecrow Press, 1994.

Chapter 5

Before and After Disasters: Federal Funding for Cultural Institutions. Washington, DC: Heritage Preservation, 2005. http://www.heritagepreservation.org/catalog.

Center, Clark, Jr., and Donnelly Lancaster, eds. *Security in Special Collections: SPEC Kit 284.* Washington, DC: Association of Research Libraries, 2004.

Field Guide to Emergency Response: A Vital Tool for Cultural Institutions. Washington, DC: Heritage Preservation, 2006. http://www.heritagepreservation.org/catalog.

Fleischer, S. Victor, and Mark J. Heppner. "Disaster Planning for Libraries and Archives: What You Need to Know and How to Do It." *Library & Archival Security* 22, no. 2 (2009): 125–140.

Forde, Helen. *Preserving Archives.* London: Facet Publishing, 2007.

Guide to Navigating FEMA and SBA Disaster Aid for Cultural Institutions. Washington, DC: Heritage Preservation, 2009. http://www.heritagepreservation.org/catalog.

Halsted, Deborah D., Richard P. Jasper, and Felicia M. Little. *Disaster Planning.* New York: Neal-Schuman Publishers, 2005.

Hunter, Gregory S. *Developing and Maintaining Practical Archives.* New York: Neal-Schuman Publishers, 2003.

Matthews, Graham, and John Feather, eds. *Disaster Management for Libraries and Archives.* Hampshire, UK: Ashgate Publishing, 2003.

Newman, John, and Walter Jones, eds. *Moving Archives: The Experiences of Eleven Archivists.* Lanham, MD: Scarecrow Press, 2002.

Pacifico, Michele F., and Thomas P. Wilsted. *Archival and Special Collections Facilities: Guidelines for Archivists, Librarians, Architects, and Engineers.* Chicago: Society of American Archivists, 2009.

Patkus, Beth Lindblom, and Karen Motylewski. "Disaster Planning." Northwest Document Conservation Center Preservation Leaflet 3.3. http://www.nedcc.org/resources/leaflets/3Emergency_Management/03DisasterPlanning.php.

Ritzenthaler, Mary Lynn. *Preserving Archives and Manuscripts*, 2nd ed. Chicago: Society of American Archivists, 2010.

Trinkaus-Randall, Gregor. *Protecting Your Collections: A Manual of Archival Security.* Chicago: Society of American Archivists, 1995.

Wellheiser, Johanna, and Jude Scott. *An Ounce of Prevention: Integrated Disaster Planning for Archives, Libraries, and Record Centers,* 2nd ed. Toronto, Ontario: Canadian Archives Foundation; Lanham, MD: Scarecrow Press, 2002.

Wilsted, Thomas. *Planning New and Remodeled Archival Facilities.* Chicago: Society of American Archivists, 2007.

Working with Emergency Responders: Tips for Cultural Institutions. Washington, DC: Heritage Preservation, 2009. http://www.heritagepreservation.org/catalog.

Chapter 6

Behrnd-Klodt, Menzi L. *Navigating Legal Issues in Archives.* Chicago: Society of American Archivists, 2008.

Burke, Frank G. *Research and the Manuscript Tradition.* Chicago: Society of American Archivists & Scarecrow Press, 1997.

Duff, Wendy, and Allyson Fox. "You're a Guide Rather Than an Expert: Archival Reference from an Archivists' Point of View." *Journal of the Society of Archivists* 27, no. 22 (2006): 129–153.

"Exhibit Makeovers: Do-It-Yourself Exhibit Planning." *History News,* American Association for State and Local History, leaflet 249, 2010. http://aaslh.org/leaflets.htm.

Finch, Elsie T. Freeman. *Advocating Archives: An Introduction to Public Relations for Archivists.* Chicago: Society of American Archivists & Scarecrow Press, 1994.

Hackman, Larry J. *Many Happy Returns: Advocacy and the Development of Archives.* Chicago: Society of American Archivists, 2011.

Hirtle, Peter B. *Copyright and Cultural Institutions: Guidelines for Digitization for U.S. Libraries, Archives, and Museums.* Ithaca, NY: Cornell University Libraries, 2009.

Kalfatovic, Martin R. *Creating a Winning Online Exhibition: A Guide for Libraries, Archives, and Museums.* Chicago: American Libraries Association, 2002.

Kurtz, Michael J. *Managing Archival & Manuscript Repositories.* Chicago: Society of American Archivists, 2004.

Mackay, Nancy. *Curating Oral Histories: From Interview to Archive.* Walnut Creek, CA: Left Coast Press, 2006.

MacNeil, Heather. *Without Consent: The Ethics of Disclosing Personal Information in Public Archives.* Chicago: Society of American Archivists & Scarecrow Press, 1992.

Mercier, Laurie, and Madeline Buckendorf. *Using Oral History in Community History Projects*. Rock Springs, WY: Oral History Association, 2007.

Murray, Keeley. "The Future of Archival Reference: Services, Technology, and Trends." *Journal for the Society of North Carolina Archivists* 7, no. 2 (2010): 26–40.

Neuenschwander, John A. *A Guide to Oral History and the Law*. (New York City) Oxford University Press, 2009.

Pugh, Mary Jo. *Providing Reference Services for Archives and Manuscripts*. Archival Fundamentals Series II. Chicago: Society of American Archivists, 2005.

Ritchie, Donald A. *Doing Oral History: A Practical Guide*, 2nd ed. Oxford: Oxford University Press, 2003.

Serrell, Beverly. *Exhibit Labels: An Interpretive Approach*. Walnut Creek, CA: AltaMira Press, 1996.

Sommer, Barbara W., and May Kay Quinlan. *The Oral History Manual*. Walnut Creek, CA: AltaMira Press, 2002.

Theimer, Kate. *Introduction to Web 2.0 in Archives . . . Or What You Need to Know in a Nutshell*. (CD-ROM). Chicago: Society of American Archivists, 2009.

———. *Web 2.0 Tools and Strategies for Archives and Local History Collections*. New York: Neal-Schuman Publishers, 2010.

Yakel, Elizabeth. *Starting an Archives*. Chicago: Society of American Archivists; Metuchen, NJ: Scarecrow Press, 1994.

Chapter 7

Dowd, Nancy. *Bite-Sized Marketing: Realistic Solutions for the Overworked Librarian*. Chicago: American Library Association, 2010.

Finch, Elsie T. Freeman. *Advocating Archives: An Introduction to Public Relations for Archivists*. Chicago: Society of American Archivists, 1994.

Konzak, Elizabeth, and Dwain P. Teague. "Reconnect with Your Alumni and Connect to Donors." *Technical Services Quarterly* 26.3 (2009): 217–225.

Kurtz, Michael J. *Managing Archival & Manuscript Repositories*. Chicago: Society of American Archivists, 2004.

Lalli, William R., ed. *Handbook of Budgeting*, 5th ed. New York: John Wiley and Sons, 2003.

Primer, Ben. "Resources for Archives: Developing Collections, Constituents, Colleagues, and Capital." *Journal of Archival Organization* 7, no. 1/2 (2009): 58–65.

Read, Sally Gardner, Beth Nawalinski, and Alexander Patterson. *101+ Great Ideas for Libraries and Friends: Marketing, Fundraising, Friends Development, and More.* New York: Neal-Schuman Publishers, 2004.

Rettig, Patricia J. "Water Tables: A Case Study of a Successful Archival Fund-Raising Event." *American Archivist* 73 (Spring/Summer 2010): 204–218.

Steele, Victoria, and Stephen D. Elder. *Becoming a Fundraiser: The Principles and Practice of Library Development*, 2nd ed. Chicago: American Libraries Association, 2000.

Vinter, Robert, and Rhea K. Kish. *Budgeting for Not-for-Profit Organizations.* New York: Free Press, 2002.

Resources Guide

The following information is organized by listing networking sources alphabetically nationally and regionally. Following those sources are lists of online manuals specifically geared toward lone arrangers. Finally, the remaining entries are listed alphabetically by topic and are broken down into subcategories, which are also listed alphabetically.

The information provided in this guide contains general information and does not include every resource available to archivists due to lack of space and time to compile such a list. Although there are many resources currently available, there will be new ones generated subsequent to this publication. All URLs and information listed below are accurate as of June 1, 2011. For a more current list of resources, consult the Society of American Archivists' Lone Arrangers Roundtable website.

Networking Sources

National Organizations

American Association of Museums (AAM)
1575 Eye Street, NW
Suite 400
Washington, DC 20005
Phone: (202) 289–1818
Fax: (202) 289–6578
http://www.aam-us.org/

American Association for State and Local History (AASLH)
1717 Church Street
Nashville, TN 37203
Phone: (615) 320–3203
Fax: (615) 327–9013
E-mail: membership@AASLH.org
http://www.aaslh.org/

Association of College and Research Libraries (ACRL)
Rare Books and Manuscripts Section (RBMS)
http://www.rbms.info/
E-mail: editor@rbms.info

Association for Recorded Sound Collections (ARSC)

Peter Shambarger

Executive Director, ARSC

P.O. Box 543

Annapolis, MD 21404

E-mail: execdir@arsc-audio.org

http://www.arsc-audio.org/

Council of State Archivists (CoSA)

308 East Burlington Street

#189

Iowa City, IA 52240

E-mail: info@statearchivists.org

http://www.statearchivists.org/

National Association of Government Archives and Records Managers (NAGARA)

Membership & Publication Services

NAGARA

1450 Western Avenue

Suite 101

Albany, NY 12203

Phone: (518) 694–8472

Fax: (518) 463–8656

E-mail: nagara@caphill.com

http://www.nagara.org

Oral History Association (OHA)

E-mail: oha@dickinson.edu

http://www.oralhistory.org/

Society of American Archivists (SAA)

17 North State Street

Suite 1425

Chicago, IL 60602

Phone: (312) 606–0722

Fax: (312) 606–0728

Toll-free: (866) 722–7858

http://www2.archivists.org/

Society of American Archivists—Lone Arrangers Roundtable

http://www.archivists.org/saagroups/lonearr/index.asp

Regional Archival/Museum/Historical Organizations

Archivists Round Table of Metropolitan New York
http://www.nycarchivists.org/

Conference of Inter-Mountain Archivists
http://cimarchivists.org/

Consortium of Iowa Archivists
http://iowaarchivists.wordpress.com/

Delaware Valley Archivists Group
http://dvarchivists.org/

Kansas City Area Archivists
http://www.kcarchivists.org/

The Kentucky Council on Archives
http://kyarchivists.org/

Michigan Archival Association
http://miarchivists.wordpress.com/

Mid-Atlantic Regional Archivists
http://www.marac.info/

Midwest Archives Conference
http://www.midwestarchives.org/

New England Archivists
http://newenglandarchivists.org/

New Hampshire Archives Group
http://www.nharchivesgroup.org/

Northwest Archivists, Inc.
http://northwestarchivistsinc.wildapricot.org/

Society of Alabama Archivists
http://www.alarchivists.org/

Society of California Archivists
http://www.calarchivists.org/

Society of Florida Archivists
http://www.florida-archivists.org/

Society of Georgia Archivists
http://soga.org/

Society of Indiana Archivists
http://www.inarchivists.org/

Society of Mississippi Archivists
http://www.msarchivists.org/

Society of North Carolina Archivists
http://www.ncarchivists.org/

Society of Ohio Archivists
http://www.ohioarchivists.org/

Society of Rocky Mountain Archivists
http://www.srmarchivists.org/

Society of Southwest Archivists
http://southwestarchivists.org/

Society of Tennessee Archivists
http://www.tennesseearchivists.org/

South Carolina Archival Association
http://www.scarchivists.org

State Historical Records Advisory Boards
http://www.statearchivists.org/shrabs.htm

Online Discussion Forums

Lone Arrangers on BigTent
https://www.bigtent.com/groups/lonearranger

The Lone Arrangers on Facebook
http://www.facebook.com/group.php?gid=8837521468&v=wall

Society of American Archivists Lone Arrangers Listserv
http://www.archivists.org/saagroups/lonearr/index.asp

Online Manuals and Resources for Lone Arrangers

A Manual for Small Archives
http://aabc.ca/media/6069/manualforsmallarchives.pdf

Archives Association of British Columbia "Archivists' Toolkit"
(This is unrelated to the open source management software developed in the United States.)
http://aabc.ca/resources/archivists-toolkit/

Arrangement & Description

Example Processing Manual
http://www.library.yale.edu/beinecke/manuscript/process/index.html

Linear Footage Calculator
http://www.library.yale.edu/beinecke/manuscript/process/lconv.htm

South Carolina State University Historical Collection Processing Manual
http://library.scsu.edu/Archives/processingmanual.pdf

Special Collections in ARL Libraries: A Discussion Report
This report talks about ways to collect and preserve materials to make them more accessible to the public. This includes traditional archival material as well as electronic material.
http://www.arl.org/bm~doc/scwg-report.pdf

Continuing Education

(See also Regional Archival/Museum/Historical Organizations.)

American Association for State and Local History Workshops
http://www.aaslh.org/workshop.htm

Amigos Library Services Continuing Education
http://www.amigos.org/node/218

Basics of Archives Continuing Education
http://www.statearchivists.org/arc/bace/index.htm

Council of State Archivists (CoSA) Resource Center
http://rc.statearchivists.org/

Educational Programs Offered by State Archives
http://www.coshrc.org/arc/education/edprogs-profarch.htm

LYRASIS—Classes and Events
http://www.lyrasis.org/Classes-and-Events.aspx

New York State Archives Training
http://www.archives.nysed.gov/a/workshops/index.shtml

Northeast Document Conservation Center—Education
http://www.nedcc.org/education/training.calendar.php

Northern Michigan University Archives—Courses and Workshops
http://webb.nmu.edu/Archives/SiteSections/CoursesAndWorkshops/Courses.html

Rare Book School

http://www.rarebookschool.org/

Rare Books and Manuscripts Section (RBMS)
http://www.rbms.info/

Society of American Archivists (SAA)
http://saa.archivists.org/Scripts/4Disapi.dll/4DCGI/events/ConferenceList.html?Action=GetEvents

UW-Madison, SLIS Continuing Education Services
http://www.slis.wisc.edu/continueed.htm

Copyright and Other Legal Issues

Copyright Term in the Public Domain in the United States
http://copyright.cornell.edu/resources/publicdomain.cfm

Digital Copyright Slider
http://www.librarycopyright.net/digitalslider/

Library Law Blog
http://blog.librarylaw.com/ (See also http://www.librarylaw.com)

Disaster Planning

Heritage Preservation
http://www.heritagepreservation.org/lessons/

LYRASIS Disaster Resources
http://www.lyrasis.org/Products-and-Services/Digital-and-Preservation-Services/Disaster-Resources.aspx

Northeast Document Conservation Center—Disaster Assistance—dPlan
http://www.nedcc.org/disaster/dplan.php

Financial Resources

Fundraising

Michigan State University Libraries—Fundraiser/Grant Writing Consultants
http://staff.lib.msu.edu/harris23/grants/fraisers.htm

Portico—Web Resources for Advancement Professionals
http://indorgs.virginia.edu/portico/

Grants

Cataloging Hidden Special Collections and Archives—Available through the Council on Library and Information Resources (CLIR), this grant is a national program to identify and catalog hidden special collections and archives. Funding can range from $75,000 to $500,000. http://www.clir.org/hiddencollections/index.html

Foundation Grants for Preservation in Libraries, Archives, and Museums—A collaborative project of the Library of Congress and the Foundation Center. This publication lists 1,725 grants of $5,000 or more awarded by 474 foundations, from 2003 through 2007. It covers grants to public, academic, research, school, and special libraries and to archives and museums for activities related to conservation and preservation. http://www.loc.gov/preservation/about/foundtn-grants.pdf

Grants—Archives.gov
http://www.archives.gov/grants/

Institute for Museum and Library Services (IMLS) Grants
http://www.imls.gov/

Library Grants and Funding from LibraryWorks.com
http://www.libraryworks.com/LW_Grants/GrantsCurrent.aspx

Maine State Archives Grant Opportunities and Forms
http://www.maine.gov/sos/arc/mhrab/grants.html

New York State Archives and Grant Opportunities
http://www.archives.nysed.gov/a/grants/index.shtml

Preservation Assistance Grants for Smaller Institutions—Available through the National Endowment for the Humanities (NEH), this grant is designed for small and mid-sized institutions, such as libraries, museums, historical societies, archival repositories, arts and cultural organizations, town and county records offices, and colleges and universities, to improve their ability to preserve and care for their humanities collections. Funding is available up to $6,000 with no match required.
http://www.neh.gov/grants/guidelines/pag.html

Texas State Libraries and Archives Commission Grants
http://www.tsl.state.tx.us/ld/funding/index.html

Tennessee State Library and Archives Grants
http://www.state.tn.us/tsla/lps/grants/grants.htm

Grant Writing

The Foundation Center (includes workshops, webinars, publications, and many other resources)
http://foundationcenter.org

Nonprofit Guides: Grant-Writing Tools for Nonprofit Organizations
http://www.npguides.org/index.html

Successful Grant Writing—Part 1: Grant Writing for Humanities, Archives, and Library Science
http://vimeo.com/12593597

Information Technology Issues

Archival Collections Management Systems

Adlib Software
http://www.adlibsoft.com/

Archivists Toolkit
http://www.archiviststoolkit.org

Archon
http://www.archon.org

Cuadra STAR
http://www.cuadra.com

Eloquent Systems
http://www.eloquent-systems.com/products/archives.shtml

PastPerfect
http://www.museumsoftware.com

Re:discovery
http://www.rediscov.com

Archival Software

"Archival Management Software: A Report for the Council on Library and Information Resources" (Council on Library and Information Resources, 2009) by Lisa Spiro
This report outlines the features of many archives management systems and discusses the advantages and tradeoffs of each application.
http://www.clir.org/pubs/reports/spiro2009.html

Archival management system features matrix (brief and full)
http://www.clir.org/pubs/reports/spiro/append2.htm
http://www.clir.org/pubs/reports/spiro/append3.htm

Archival Software Wiki
http://archivalsoftware.pbworks.com/

Archivists' Toolkit matrix of Archivists' Toolkit, Archon, and PastPerfect features
http://archiviststoolkit.org/node/76

ICA Study 12—Market Survey of Commercially Available Off-the-Shelf Archival Management Software, 2003
http://www.ica.org/ (search: "archival management software")

The Museum Association of New York—Collections Management Software
http://manyonline.org/resources/collections-management-software/

Digital Asset Management Systems

Comparison of Digital Asset Management Systems—University of North Texas
http://digital.library.unt.edu/ark:/67531/metadc29818/

ContentDM
http://www.contentdm.org

Digital Asset Management News
http://digitalassetmanagementnews.org/

Digital Asset Management (DAM) Planning/Implementation Survey (8/1/10–8/31/10) conducted by the University of Connecticut Libraries
http://digitalcommons.uconn.edu/libr_pubs/24/

Greenstone
http://www.greenstone.org

Luna Insight
http://www.lunaimaging.com/insight/index.html

Museums and Online Archives Collaboration Digital Asset Management Database
http://www.bampfa.berkeley.edu/moac/

Museolog
http://museolog.unesco.kz/i.php?q=museolog

OpenText
http://digitalmedia.opentext.com/default.aspx

Digitization

Building Digital Collections: A Technical Overview from the Library of Congress American Memory project
http://memory.loc.gov/ammem/about/techIn.html

Do It Yourself Digitization from an Archivist's Perspective (Blog)
http://www.mistydemeo.com/

Federal Agencies Digitization Guidelines Initiatives
http://www.digitizationguidelines.gov/

NINCH Guide to Good Practice in the Digital Representation and Management of Cultural Heritage Materials
http://www.nyu.edu/its/humanities/ninchguide/

Society of American Archivists Annual Conference, Washington, DC, 2010 SESSION 107—Real World Digitizing for Humble Shops Undertaking Hefty Digitization Projects
http://saa.archivists.org/Scripts/4Disapi.dll/4DCGI/events/eventdetail.
html?Action=Events_Detail&Time=899652118&InvID_W=1427

Encoded Archival Description (EAD)

EAD Help Pages (SAA EAD Roundtable)
http://www.archivists.org/saagroups/ead/index.html

EAD Templates

http://bentley.umich.edu/EAD/bhlfiles.php

Northwest Digital Archives Best Practice Guidelines for EAD

http://nwda.orbiscascade.org/best_practices/intro.html

OAC Best Practice Guidelines for EAD

http://www.cdlib.org/services/dsc/contribute/docs/oacbpgead_v2-0.pdf

Official EAD Version 2002 Website

http://www.loc.gov/ead/

Yale University EAD Encoding Best Practice Guidelines

http://www.library.yale.edu/facc/bpgs.html

Institutional Repositories

Digital Commons

http://digitalcommons.bepress.com/

DSpace

http://www.dspace.org

EPrints

http://www.eprints.org/software/

Fedora

http://www.fedoraproject.org

Institutional Repositories Webinar Series

http://www.ala.org/ala/mgrps/divs/alcts/confevents/upcoming/webinar/irs/index.cfm

IR+

http://www.irplus.org

Metadata

Introduction to Metadata

http://www.getty.edu/research/publications/electronic_publications/intrometadata/

Metadata and Cataloging Resources

https://pantherfile.uwm.edu/mll/www/resource.html

Metadata: Minnesota State Archives

http://www.mnhs.org/preserve/records/metadata.html

North Carolina: Exploring Cultural Heritage Online (ECHO) Chapter 5: Metadata

http://www.ncecho.org/documents/5metadata_2007.pdf

Understanding Metadata
http://www.niso.org/publications/press/UnderstandingMetadata.pdf

Preservation & Conservation Services

American Institute for Conservation
http://www.conservation-us.org

AMIGOS Imaging and Preservation Service (APS)
http://www.amigos.org/node/45

CALIPR Preservation Planning Tool
http://sunsite.berkeley.edu/CALIPR/index.html

Canadian Conservation Institute
http://www.cci-icc.gc.ca/index-eng.aspx

Conservation Center for Art and Historic Artifacts
http://www.ccaha.org

Heritage Preservation
http://www.heritagepreservation.org/

ICA Art Conservation
http://www.ica-artconservation.org/

Massachusetts Board of Library Commissioners Preservation Resources
http://mblc.state.ma.us/advisory/preservation/resources.php

Library of Congress Preservation
http://www.loc.gov/preserv/

Midwest Art Conservation Center
http://www.preserveart.org/

Northeast Document Conservation Center
http://www.nedcc.org/resources/introduction.php

Preservation Advisory Centre at the British Library
http://www.bl.uk/blpac/publicationsleaf.html

Preservation and Archives Professionals
http://www.archives.gov/preservation/

Digital Preservation

Digital Curation and Preservation Bibliography
http://digital-scholarship.org/dcpb/dcpb.htm

Digital Curation Reference Manual
http://www.dcc.ac.uk/resources/curation-reference-manual

Digital Preservation Education for North Carolina State Government Employees

(The information contained on this site can apply to the general public.)

http://digitalpreservation.ncdcr.gov/

Program Planning

Archival Needs Assessment

http://www.archives.nysed.gov/a/records/mr_pub59_accessible.html

InternActive

http://internactive.org

Records Management

Association for Information and Image Management (AIIM)

1100 Wayne Avenue

Suite 1100

Silver Spring, MD 20910

Phone: (301) 587–8202

Toll-free: (800) 477–2446

E-mail: aiim@aiim.org

http://www.aiim.org/

ARMA International

11880 College Boulevard

Suite 450

Overland Park, KS 66210

Phone: (913) 341–3808

Toll-free: (800) 422–2762

Fax: (913) 341–3742

http://www.arma.org/

Federal Information and Records Managers Council (FIRM)

http://firmcouncil.org/

Information Requirements Clearinghouse

5600 S. Quebec Street

Suite 250C

Greenwood Village, CO 80111

Phone: (303) 721–7500

E-mail: info@irch.com

http://www.irch.com

Iron Mountain—Knowledge Center

http://www.ironmountain.com/knowledge-center/knowledgecenter-home.html

National Archives and Records Administration—Resources for Records Managers

http://www.archives.gov/records-mgmt/

New York State Archives—Managing Records

http://www.archives.nysed.gov/a/records/index.shtml

Records Management Today Podcast Series

http://nuweb.northumbria.ac.uk/ceis_podcasts/index.php

Society of Rocky Mountain Archivists—Records Management Basics

http://www.srmarchivists.org/index.php?q=content/records-management-basics

Electronic Records Management

ICA Archival Automation Bibliography, December 2002

http://www.ica.org/8151/public-resources/archival-automation-ica-bibliography-1.html

International Records Management Trust—Additional Resources for Electronic Records Management

http://www.irmt.org/researchReports.php

Minnesota State Archives—Electronic Records Management

http://www.mnhs.org/preserve/records/electronicrecords.htm

Practical E-Records—blog by Chris Prom

http://e-records.chrisprom.com/

About the Author

Christina Zamon is the head of Archives and Special Collections at Emerson College in Boston, Massachusetts. Prior to that she was the archivist for the National Press Club, a cataloging assistant for retrospective conversion at the Frick Art Reference Library in New York City, and an acquisitions assistant at the Folger Shakespeare Library in Washington, D.C., where she procured rare books and manuscripts. She holds dual master's degrees in library science and history from the University of Maryland where she also worked as a graduate assistant in the Preservation Department. In 2005 she became a Certified Archivist. Zamon's professional activities include serving as chair of the Lone Arrangers Roundtable of the Society of American Archivists from 2010–2012 and active membership in the New England Archivists. Zamon is the co-founder of the original Lone Arrangers social networking site on Ning and now Big Tent.

Case Study Contributors

Barbara Austen is the archivist at the Connecticut Historical Society (CHS) in Hartford, Connecticut. She holds an MA in history from the College of William and Mary and an MLIS from Simmons College. She is an active member of the New England Archivists and serves on the Connecticut State Historical Records Advisory Board and on several subcommittees of the board. Most recently, she and the staff at CHS wrote two successful NHPRC grant proposals, the first to reduce the cataloging backlog and the second to nearly eliminate it.

Terry Baxter has been an archivist at the Multnomah County (Oregon) Records Program since 1998. He has been an archivist for nearly twenty-five years, previously at the Oregon State Archives and at Pacificorp. He has served in a variety of elected and appointed positions in the Society of American Archivists and Northwest Archivists and has been a member of the Academy of Certified Archivists since 2004. He lives in Portland, Oregon, and blogs at *Beaver Archivist*.

Michelle Ganz is currently a lone arranger at the Lincoln Memorial University and the Abraham Lincoln Library and Museum in Tennessee. She received her BA in medieval literature from The Ohio State University in 2003 and her MLIS from the University of Arizona in 2006. In 2008 she became a member of the Academy of Certified Archivists. She is currently active in both the Society of American Archivists and the Academy of Certified Archivists.

Russell L. Gasero is archivist for the Reformed Church in America (RCA) in New Brunswick, New Jersey, and has been an archivist since 1973 and a lone arranger since 1978. He began his experiment in archival work at the United Nations Archives before starting the RCA Archives. He has served as chair of the Archivists of Religious Collections Section and was co-founder and co-chair of the Lone Arrangers Roundtable, both in the Society of American Archivists and as the chair of the Archivists of Religious Institutions regional archival organization. Gasero has presented papers and led workshops numerous times at SAA, the Mid-Atlantic Regional Archives Conference, the American Association for State and Local History, and other organizations and has published articles and books on archives and Reformed Church history.

Tamara Gaydos has served as the archivist at the Phillips Library at the Peabody Essex Museum in Salem, Massachusetts, since 2007. She holds a BS in Russian from Georgetown University and an MLIS from Simmons College. She is an active member of the New England Archivists and Society of American Archivists. Her archival career includes time spent at the Beverly (Mass.) Historical Society, Steven Phillips Memorial Trust House, and Northeastern University.

Jeremy Linden is preservation environment specialist at the Image Permanence Institute (IPI), Rochester Institute of Technology, in Rochester, New York. He is primarily involved in the environmental management activities of IPI and works closely with colleagues in libraries, archives, and museums on issues of material preservation, mechanical system performance, energy saving, and sustainability. Formerly head of archives and special collections at the State University of New York at Fredonia, Linden earned an MLS in information studies and an MA in history from the University of Maryland and a BA in history from Vassar College.

Meg Miner is university archivist and special collections librarian and assistant professor at Illinois Wesleyan University (IWU). She works with American studies, history, and nursing faculty to build library collections and assists students with research needs and instruction. She established a records management program at IWU in 2008, helping to build an institutional repository in 2009 that now includes active deposits from major IWU committees. In 2010 the IR took in the first electronically deposited research honors theses at IWU. Her research interests encompass the impact digital collections are having on scholarship, environmentally friendly library practices, and the role archives play in memory instruction.

Christina Prucha is the cataloger and archivist for the Learning Resource Center at Logan College of Chiropractic, St. Louis, Missouri. She received her MLS from the University of Arizona and is a Certified Archivist. She was the archivist of the American Choral Directors Association from 2006–2010. Under her direction, the archives moved 90 miles from Lawton, Oklahoma, to its present home in Oklahoma City. With the help of two library school interns, she organized the

800-linear-feet of material and created finding aids with the help of Archivists' Toolkit. Outreach from the archives was and remains one of her passions, and she is always looking for ways to promote archival use.

Peg Poeschl Siciliano has been the archivist at the History Center of Traverse City (formerly the Traverse Area Historical Society) in Traverse City, Michigan, since 2006. She received her MA in American history with a specialty in archives from the College of William and Mary in 1986. Her archival career includes time spent at the Nebraska State Historical Society, the Russian Orthodox Church in America, and the Con Foster Museum in Traverse City. She was also co-director of the Fading Memories Project, an archival education project funded, in part, by the Michigan Humanities Council. In 2010 she focused on enabling a group of dedicated volunteers to run a first-class, professional-caliber manuscripts repository on a very limited budget. She believes that local history collections can be the basic building blocks of the entire historical profession and is dedicated to strengthening that foundation.

John H. Slate is the archivist for the City of Dallas, where he is responsible for historic city government records in the Dallas Municipal Archives. He is a member of the Academy of Certified Archivists and possesses a BS from the University of Texas at Austin and an MLIS, specializing in archival enterprise, from the same institution. His work in archives, libraries, and special collections began at the Center for American History at the University of Texas at Austin, where he spent thirteen years. He previously was curator/librarian at the Hertzberg Museum of the San Antonio Public Library and was archivist at the Texas African American Photography Archive in Dallas. He is past chair of the Government Records and the Visual Materials Sections and served as president of the Society of Southwest Archivists from 2010 to 2011. In addition, he is a member of the Texas State Library and Archives' Historical Records Advisory Board.

Alison Stankrauff is the campus archivist and an associate librarian at Indiana University South Bend, where she inherited an archives that had not had an archivist for ten years. She created all of the archives' policies and made outreach one of her primary goals. Since her arrival in 2004, reference requests have grown exponentially, much to her gratification. She previously served as a reference archivist at the American Jewish Archives and as a technician at the Reuther Labor Archives at Wayne State University, where she earned her MLS with a concentration in archival administration in 2002. She holds a BA in history from Antioch College.

Nicole L. Thaxton is the corporate archivist for Caterpillar Inc. She obtained an MLIS from the University of Illinois at Champaign-Urbana in 1995 and became a certified archivist in 2006. She worked as a reference librarian for five years before accepting her current position in 2000.

Index

BOLD indicates illustrations